Song Arrangement for the Small Recording Studio

Amos Clarke

Song Arrangement for the Small Recording Studio

Revision 1 – Published January 17, 2016.
Song Arrangement for the Small Recording Studio
Copyright 2016 - All Rights Reserved – Amos P. W. Clarke

ALL RIGHTS RESERVED.
No part of this publication may be reproduced or transmitted in any form whatsoever, electronic, or mechanical, including photocopying, recording, or by any informational storage or retrieval system without express written, dated and signed permission from the author.

Contents

Who is this book for?	1
Why you should read this book	3
How to get maximum value from this book	5
1 What is song arrangement?	7
2 Why is arrangement so important?	11
3 The Formula	14
4 Complexity	21
5 Structure	28
6 Dynamics	36
7 Transitions	43
8 Builds	50
9 Groove	57
10 The Hook	62
11 Tempo and duration	69
12 Establishing the Lead	75
13 Clarity and definition	83
14 Symmetry and repetition	103
15 Comparison and analysis	113
16 Checklist	118
17 Glossary	121
Thanks	125
Other books by the author	126

Song Arrangement for the Small Recording Studio

Who is this book for?

This book is intended for recording engineers, musicians, songwriters and producers who want to learn more about song arrangement. The book is intended for those with all levels of experience.

The information in this book is not an authority on song arrangement. It is a culmination of ideas, rules, principles and concepts developed by the author from over 20 years of song-writing, performance, production and mixing. While all of the material is intended to be original, some of it is developed and expanded upon from already accepted methodology.

You don't need to have an in-depth understanding of music to understand and apply the theory in this book. You don't need to be able to read and write music notation or create orchestral scores. It's written in plain language (OK, there's a bit of jargon here and there) and there's a glossary at the rear to help if you get stuck on any of the terminology. This book won't make you an instant and overnight expert on arrangement. However, applying the principles and developing your own ideas, along with LOTS of hours of experience and practical application, probably will.

This book focuses on arrangement techniques for predominantly popular music styles. At the end of this book, you should be prepared with a range of knowledge and skills that you can apply to real projects.

A great song relies on a great arrangement

Why you should read this book

If you're looking for a way to improve the quality of your song recordings, then this book is for you. If you're tired of reading countless books on mixing techniques in an effort to improve your music productions, then again, this book is for you. Understanding and applying the principles of good arrangement could be the secret sauce for crafting that perfect mix.

For many years I focused on mixing strategies and processing techniques (compression, EQ, FX etc.) as a means to achieving that pro sound in my music productions, but there still seemed to be something missing. After many years it became clear that arrangement was a critical factor that could significantly improve the quality of my mixes.

In other words, having a great mix relies on having a great song. All the technical skills and gear in the world will only get you part of the way toward creating that awesome song recording. Even a great recording and wonderful performance will not be enough if you don't have a great song to start with. In this context, the definition of a 'great song' is great lyrics, great music and a great arrangement. While many of us are good at mixing, lyric writing and making music, the arrangement so often seems to be a missing ingredient.

This book is aimed at helping you understand concepts and principles of song arrangement and gives you ways to apply the skills in your own music. The information presented in this book regularly crosses over into composition and production territory. While producer and arranger are two distinct roles in the song creation process, each can blend and include elements of the other. What a wonderful marriage!

This book works on the basis that crafting a great arrangement can transform even the most mediocre of songs into something special.

Good arrangement is a critical part of crafting that perfect song recording

How to get maximum value from this book

Each chapter in this book ends with a section called 'Application'. These are designed to summarise each chapter and to help you apply the theory in a practical way into your own song projects. In the past my readers have told me they like this approach because it helped them actually do something useful with the information. I hope you find value in this approach.

A Song Arrangement Checklist is included at the end of the book. You can use this template as a way to methodically apply important principles into your own songs. Using a checklist/template on a regular basis ensures consistency in the quality of your work – don't underestimate its value.

I recommend using this book as a reference that you can review regularly. There's a lot of content covered and a lot for readers to assimilate in one read.

I sincerely hope that from reading this book, you achieve an understanding of these principles and techniques, and use them as a spring-board to develop your own. Most of all, I hope you get a break-through in your own ability to craft great songs.

Let's get started.

Arrangement is very much about the manipulation of patterns and repetition

1
What is song arrangement?

The organisation of musical elements and sections in a musical composition with the aim of creating a pleasing listening experience for the intended audience

A basic overview of arrangement

One of the most important aspects of arrangement is that it is almost entirely about the manipulation of musical patterns. The organisation of Verses, Choruses and other sections involves a series of repeating patterns. Within each pattern of sections reside further patterns created by the turnarounds and phrasing of drum rhythms, bass lines, Lead vocals and the like. A great arranger knows when to repeat a pattern, vary a pattern and change to a new pattern. The sole aim of this shuffling and organisation of patterns is to create a great sounding song; one that delivers an emotional message; one that keeps people on the dance-floor; one that keeps listeners listening and coming back for more.

The goal of arrangement is to tell a dynamic and compelling story

A great arrangement will draw the listener in and captivate them until the end. The musical story would effectively convey the emotion intended by the composer; happy or sad, aggressive or submissive, acceptance or denial – the list goes on. Ideally, your listeners will hum, whistle or sing the Hook and won't be able to get the song out of their head. They will want to listen again and they'll tell their friends about it. From a commercial aspect, you hope they'll buy it and that it may achieve some level of success on radio, the internet, or whatever distribution is targeted.

The arranger is architect of the composition

Arrangement is about organisation and structure, and the creation and manipulation of musical patterns. An architect has control over a building's structure and aesthetics; they create rhythm by the repetition of visual elements and create a user environment based on the selection and combination of materials. Similarly, an arranger is in control of maintaining listener interest, conveying emotion, controlling dynamics, energy, duration, focus and pace.

The musical environment they create is ideally one that listeners want to come back to. Their skills can bring out the best in a performance, turning a bunch of lyrics and musical progressions into story, or even better, a musical journey.

Decisions made by the arranger will ultimately affect the clarity of the final song recording due to the selection and placement (both panoramic and depth) of musical elements in the mix. This is achieved by limiting the number of musical elements occurring at any one time, and retaining only those elements that contribute in a meaningful way – more about this in the chapter, Clarity and Definition.

Think of the listener as a diner who gets a wonderful epicurean experience

The diner starts with an appetising entrée that sets the scene. This is followed by the big event; a sumptuous main course. Finally, the meal is rounded off with dessert; a palate cleanser and sweet reminder of an enjoyable event. You could expand this analogy further by adding an aperitif to the start and coffee to the tail end. Taking this still further, you might consider a song to be like a degustation experience, with up to twenty courses. Pink Floyd's 'Shine on You Crazy Diamond' comes to mind here. At around 26 minute's duration, it's a feast of a song.

Let's consider the diner who's in a hurry. They bowl on into a fast-food burger joint. Long day at work. Cavernous hunger. There's no hovering around debating the menu options. They're straight in with the big-daddy burger, two litres of their favourite bubbly beverage, and they're out in three minutes. Now that's a short song that hits hard and stops dead like it's been chopped off with an axe. Adam Lynch's 'United States of Whatever' springs to mind at around 1.27 total duration.

Arrangement plays a significant part in the way a song is perceived, by enabling a way to package the structure and energy of a song into a listenable experience for the intended audience.

Arrangement is the piecing together of a puzzle of musical patterns in a pleasing order for the intended audience

2

Why is arrangement so important?

Great arrangement can transform a mediocre song into greatness and a great song into brilliance, conversely a poor arrangement can all but ruin any composition

Song arrangement affects audience listenability

The goal of any song arrangement destined for airplay is to create a production that is engaging and exciting for the intended audience; a song that will capture their interest, get them talking, and leave them wanting more.

A great song arrangement can add that touch of professional class to your songs by using proven techniques used in popular music production. Many of these principles are hidden but, upon careful analysis, are revealed as fairly simple and effective techniques. The prolific occurrence of these techniques in modern music is perhaps evidence that rules and principles are being rigorously applied, even if they're not that obvious during general listening. Some typical examples are radio format songs commonly reaching the first Chorus within 30 – 45 seconds of starting and the very common 3.30 minute duration.

When arrangement principles are ignored or poorly executed, they can negatively impact the quality of a song by confusing, boring and disengaging the listener. The good news is that applying even one or two simple rules and principles can make a tremendous difference to the palatability and listenability of a song.

Good arrangement brings out the best

There are many methods and techniques in this book that are intended to bring out the best in a song. For example, a well-arranged song creates tension and release, and a dynamic energy flow that can captivate an audience. This manipulation of energy is generated by many factors. These include such things as artist performance, pace, and the selection of instrumentation based on tonal character, to name a few.

For instance, working with a vocalist could bring out an emotionally charged performance that would really make the Chorus shine. Similarly, simplifying the rhythm section in Verses allows the players to elevate their energy in the Chorus. This combination of improvement to the vocal, drum, and bass performances could generate a high energy Chorus that contrasts perfectly with the more subdued Verses.

These are just a few examples of how the many techniques and methods of arrangement can be incorporated to improve the quality of the finished song recording.

Great arrangement may be the missing link; the Holy Grail that could take your song productions to the next level

3

The Formula

Arrangement is a vital ingredient in the creation of a great song and equally important, is knowing how it fits into the song production process

A great song recording has a success formula

Making a song is a lot like baking a cake. Average ingredients and an average process will at best, result in an average cake. If you miss one or more of the ingredients or you miss a step in the baking instructions, the likely outcome is a terrible cake.

Making a song is similar in terms of ingredients and process; miss any one and the likely result is poor or average at best. On the positive side, following a great formula will likely yield a great cake. If you were to consistently follow a successful formula, then you can bake a great cake, or song, every time.

In terms of making a great song, having a successful <u>formula</u> is the number-one thing to know. Having the best <u>ingredients</u> available is the second thing. And <u>assembling</u> it all correctly is the third. When we can get a successful trio of formula, ingredients and assembly happening, it's difficult for the results to be anything else but outstanding. When we add consistency into the mix, we start to create great songs, time after time.

In reality, getting consistent quality in all three areas is tough work. However, knowing part of the equation and making a big effort to get schooled-up in your weak areas puts you on a 'quest for success'. In other words, when you're always searching for ways to learn and improve, the outcome is almost always continued improvement.

The rest of this chapter aims to give you The Formula for creating a great song and the reasoning behind it. The rest of this book aims to provide you with the things you need to know about <u>assembly</u> for ingredient number 2.

The Formula for a great song production

The formula consists of critical key ingredients done well and in a specific order. Although the order can vary slightly, it should contain all of the ingredients. Arrangement is one of those key ingredients.

1. Great composition
Music, lyrics and story

+

2. Great arrangement
Organisation of musical elements, the structure and arrangement of musical sections, pace, focus, maintaining listener interest and more

+

3. Great performance
Good quality instruments tuned, played with expression and in time, vocals delivered with passion, emotion, pitch and phrasing

+

4. Great recording
All musical performances captured technically well including: microphone choice and placement, room tone, instrument tone, correct gain staging, preamp choice, quality of recording gear and formats

+

5. Great production – *can happen at multiple stages in The Formula*
A technical and artistic overview of each and every step in The Formula, with the goal of making a great song recording suitable for the end user and stakeholders (record company, label, radio station etc.)

+

6. Great mix and master
A well-balanced recording that captures the sound and soul of the artist/band and exhibiting best use of dynamic and delay based processing with correct loudness levels.

=

Great music recording

Each ingredient in The Formula has a critical part to play in the creation of a great song recording

+ Songwriters craft the original compositions.
+ Arrangers fine-tune the song format and arrange the musical elements.
+ Producers bring out the best performances and often do arrangement work.
+ Recording engineers capture the performances.
+ Mix engineers combine, balance and add personality to the recording.
+ And the mastering engineer puts the polish on the final mix.

A great song recording has a success formula consisting of critical key ingredients arranged in a specific order

The challenge for the 'one-man-band' studio owner

It's often difficult for small studios to do each of the necessary steps well during the song creation process. Unless you have access to a high level of skill for each ingredient in The Formula, it's likely that your final song productions will lack quality in your weak areas. If you're a one-man-band operator, having the necessary breadth and depth of skillsets at your finger-tips is difficult. If you want to create professional sounding, high quality song productions then all of the ingredients in The Formula are required and they must be done well.

Three important areas to focus on at the beginning of a project

At the beginning of any project, particular attention needs to be placed on the performance, the arrangement, and the composition. Focusing on these three areas enables you to start the arrangement process before final recording, mixing and mastering takes place. It's often tempting to move immediately to the recording phase but doing this is like a factory going into production on an untested and potentially sub-standard product. Getting these three things right early on will pay dividends later on.

1. The Performance

Definition: The quality of performance of each band member, both individually and collectively. Each member must be able to play their designated part well, while supporting the other members. The 'whole should be more than the parts'. Particular importance is placed on the Lead vocalist. Prior to recording, this is most easily done by analysing a band's demo or listening to a live performance of the song.
Things to listen for:
a. Can each member play in time?
b. Can the Lead vocalist deliver an intense/emotional/meaningful performance?
c. Can the Lead singer sing with correct pitch and phrasing?
d. Do all the instruments combine and sound good together?
e. Are any members over-playing or under-playing?
f. Does each band member allow musical 'space' for the others?
g. Overall, does the band seem to 'gel' as a unit? If not, why?

2. The Arrangement

Definition: The duration, the Time-To-Chorus, energy dynamics of the song, structure of song sections, and how engaging the song sounds.
Things to listen for:
a. Does the song have an obvious Hook?
b. Is the Hook over-used or under-used?
c. What is the format (ABABCBB)? Find out more in the 'Structure' chapter.
d. Does the song have good energy dynamics? Find out more in the 'Dynamics' chapter.
e. Does the song have a strong 'Lead'? Find out more in the 'Establishing the Lead' chapter.
f. Does the song seem too long or too short?
g. Do some musical parts clash with others, like a guitar solo over a Lead vocal?

3. The Composition

Definition: The lyrics, the message, the music, the tempo.
Things to listen for:
a. What is the song's message?
b. Do the lyrics make sense and support the message?
c. Are the harmonic relationships correct for the musical parts? Are there clashes?
d. Does the songwriter own the rights to all the music and words?

Application

1. Focus on the key ingredients
For every song you work on, focus your attention on each of the ingredients in terms of getting the best outcome for each. Get an expert involved if you're weak in one area. Be honest with yourself about whether all the ingredients have been done well.

2. Identify your strengths and weaknesses
Look at what your strengths are in terms of each ingredient in The Formula. Consider ways to develop your weaknesses: buy a book, do an online course, join an online forum, or join a group.

3. Develop your skills
Actively connect with people online and collaborate on musical projects. Sharing ideas and learning from others is a great way to improve your skills and knowledge. Check out sites like **www.indabamusic.com**, and **www.musiccollaboration.com**

4. Create a team
Form a small commercial song-writing production team consisting of people with skills in composition, arrangement and production. Create demos and sell your songs online.

5. Analyse songs
Analyse songs in your area of interest and discuss your ideas with others. Check out 'forensics of a song' on **www.musinformation.com** for an in-depth analysis of a range of songs. Also check out Bobby Owsinski's 'Deconstructed Hits' at **www.bobbyowsinski.com** where he '...takes you deep inside some of the most iconic hits of all time.'

4

Complexity

No arrangement should be more complex or less simple than it needs to be to achieve its goal

The complexity of a song affects its listenability

How complex should our arrangements be? Is complex song construction valuable for the listener or the artist? These are questions that need to be asked early on in the production process. For maximum impact, the complexity of the arrangement should be sympathetic with the genre and the intended audience. Complexity is important because the more complex the arrangements, the less accessible they become for the listener.

Simple pop songs require simple arrangements of short duration and historically, that's what makes a pop song fit the pop genre. Pop songs are short stories with simple plots that get into the action quickly. In effect, they're simple. Alternatively, progressive rock styles happily accommodate much longer and more complex arrangements because this is what the genre demands and that's what listeners expect. Similarly, jazz can be too harmonically complex for some listeners. For some genres, complexity is perfect and expected. For other genres, simplicity is what is required.

The big question is what makes a song complex or simple? Perhaps simplicity is best described as a 'less is more' approach. This means short songs, simple melodies, simple harmonic relationships (less chord changes), strong Hooks, and simple song structure. Complexity is simply the opposite of this.

Pop songs are short stories with simple plots that get into the action quickly

Let's use the example of a simple pop song arrangement. Our imaginary pop song is very easy to listen to because the song's construction consists of a limited number of sections, a common radio format, and very simple vocal melodies with a strong Hook. Additionally, our 'Hooky' Chorus comes around frequently in the song, so our listeners have a regular anchor. We even help our listeners recognise the Chorus before it comes by adding a *Transition* (a very short musical element like a drum fill or effect directly before the Chorus). On top of this, our song has the same pattern of sections duplicated two or three times throughout the song. For example, our Intro > Verse > Chorus repeats itself again and just when it gets boring, we add a Solo or Bridge, then we finish on a 'feel good' high by a coda of repeating Chorus lines. Simple!

This song is an easy listen and it appeals to lots of younger listeners who like simple short stories that get to the punch line quickly. You could say that simple pop songs can be like confectionery: bright, sweet, and with a big burst of flavour.

Simple arrangements appeal to a large range of listeners because less complexity makes a song easier to listen to. Less complexity also makes a song easier to create and arrange. However, less complex arrangements don't have to be boring and uninteresting. Short songs with simple arrangements and strong musical Hooks are likely to be more memorable because they can be catchy and easy to remember. Many mainstream radio hits fall into this category where a simple arrangement has provided a powerful and memorable listening experience.

There are countless examples of highly successful radio hits with simple arrangements. A very common trait among these songs is their short duration, memorable Hooks and powerful riffs. Green Day's 'American Idiot' has a very simple arrangement of two alternating sections injected with a guitar solo played over the music backing of one of the sections. The Spice Girls' massive hit, 'Wannabe' also has only two highly contrasting sections comprising vocal rapping over a powerful 'riffy' Verse and a very contrasting melodic Chorus.

Examples of hit songs with simple arrangements

My United States of Whatever - Liam Lynch
A very short, punchy and humorous song with a 1.27 duration consisting of two distinct and alternating sections.

Shaddap Your Face – Joe Dulce
This is another example of two simple alternating parts with a very Hooky Chorus. The song uses humour as a major element of attraction.

Gangnam Style - Psy
This song alternates between variations on a main groove and a very melodic section. Interestingly, the most melodic sections of the song are perhaps the weakest. The vocal rapping over the highly rhythmical groove and the 'Gangnam style' vocal Hook are the highlight of the song.

Simple pop songs can be like confectionery: bright and sweet with a big burst of flavour

A complex song arrangement could be described as an ever-changing organisation of varying sections in varying order and duration

The reference to 'sections' refers to Intros, Verses, Choruses and the like. The 'complex harmonic structures', refers to the contrast between transient-rich (drums) and tonal-rich (melodic) instrumentation, and the relationship of frequency dominant musical elements.

Complex song arrangement is common in classical music where there is often an intricate and multi-faceted interaction of many instruments. In addition, the extended duration and the complex structures create very interesting songs.

A complex song is like a seven-course dining experience

Think of a complex song like a 'chef's platter': pate, grapes, crunchy salty crackers, a variety of cheeses, and a small bowl of sweet and spicy plum and onion chutney. There are so many flavours, textures and aromas; complex and enjoyable and full of variety. Sounds a bit like jazz, classical, or a Pink Floyd number doesn't it?

There are many elements that make a dining experience special beyond what turns up on the plate; the quality of service, a relaxed ambience and the person you're with, for example. In terms of a complex song, it's the variety and quality of many related elements that makes the main event special. Much like a five-course meal, longer, more complex songs often need many varying elements to develop the journey. Much like our epicurean extravaganza, these kinds of songs need complex aromas, visual delights, and a variety of rich and subtle flavours.

Songs don't necessarily need to be long in duration to be complex. They can be short with complicated structures or chord progressions, or both. A simple way to create a complex song is by complicating the song structure. For example, a typical pop song has a lot of repetition; repeating patterns of Verses and regular Choruses. This same song could be made complex by ensuring that no section repeated itself. This would mean composing more sections, but you probably get the point.

An important point about simplicity versus complexity is that simple songs are easier to listen to. However, whether you're aiming for a simple or complex song, the intended audience needs to be firmly in mind.

It's not uncommon to publish a number of arrangements for different audiences. This can include the radio mix, karaoke mix, dance mix, film mix (extended with no vocals).

Examples of complex songs

Shine On You Crazy Diamond – Pink Floyd
A nine-part composition originally intended to take up one side of a vinyl record, the song has a duration of over 26 minutes. The song has long sections of Lead solo instrumental parts and very Hooky Lead vocals.

Autumn Almanac – The Kinks
This song packs in a considerable amount of melodic and structural variation in just over 3 minutes. Even with such variation, the song successfully has a natural flow from section to section.

This Whole World – The Beach Boys
This is a beautiful composition with a very complex structure all packed into a very short duration of around 2.20. However, it's difficult to feel anchored to this song due to the lack of a strong and repetitive Hook.

St. Alphonzo's Pancake Breakfast - Frank Zappa
This song is beautiful in its weirdness and complex melodic and rhythmical structure. Once again, it is the antithesis of modern pop due to its lack of simple and repetitive Hooks.

Application

1. Know your audience
Be certain on the genre and intended audience for each song you arrange. If your audience is mainstream radio, then the arrangement will need to fit certain criteria for playability. Similarly, if you're creating a compilation of café jazz songs, then the song arrangements might be more complex with longer durations.

2. Analyse a range of simple and complex songs
How much does melody, Hook and song structure contribute to a song's simplicity or complexity? Start with the examples provided above.

3. Discuss and review
Talk about song simplicity/complexity in a group or forum and read about other peoples' views and methods. Talking to professionals and learning their secrets can be liberating for your own personal development. You can find more discussions about song complexity on **www.gearslutz.com**, (songwriting section) **www.reddit.com**, **www.bobbyowsinski.com** (deconstructed hits).

4. Experiment
Experiment with a song you're working on by creating simple and complex versions of the arrangement. You can put a demo mix of the song into a simple audio editor and re-arrange the song sections (Verses/Choruses etc.). This is a useful technique for getting feedback from potential listeners about their listening preferences.

5

Structure

Song structure is about the organisation of the song's sections into a desired sequence and frequency

The arranger's goal is to assemble a pattern of sections into an enjoyable and engaging listening experience

Getting the song structure right is one of the most critical steps in the arrangement process. This is where song 'architecture' takes place; sections are organised into logical patterns that have a good balance of repetition. From here, each section can be built and sculpted to affect the intensity and energy of the song, thereby creating a dynamic flow of energy as the song progresses. For instance, it's very common to have low or medium intensity in Verses then build to more intensity in the Choruses.

The frequency, repetition, and placement of sections, is critical in achieving and maintaining listener enjoyment. This is because each song section has a role in the development of song. The introduction gives listeners an overview. The Verse prepares the audience for the Chorus. The Chorus is the song's climax. The Solo, Bridge, or Middle-8, provides variety to the repeating patterns of a typical Verse/Chorus combination.

Particular attention should be paid to the Choruses and Hooks in the song so that these are introduced at the right time and delivered in a way to hold listener attention. Waiting too long to get to the Chorus can leave the listener unsatisfied. It can also reduce the likelihood of the song being a radio hit. Similarly, over-repetition of the Chorus can 'over-cook' the song, potentially risking a monotonous production.

Sequence and frequency of sections: the art and the science

What is the best order for sections in a song? And how often should they occur? The answer to these questions comes down to art and science. The art comes from one's instinct and usually improves as your experience increases. Simply put, the more you immerse yourself in the practice of arrangement, the quicker you will begin to understand what works and what doesn't. The science, however, is more measurable. Evidence of this is in a decade's worth of radio hits and highly reviewed albums from a wide range of genres. These are all easily accessed by a simple internet search.

It's well worth the effort to analyse the structure of a hit-song because this can tell you a whole lot about what mainstream listeners actually like. A great place to start is with your own personal favourites. Try doing a comparative analysis of hit songs over several decades, comparing a range of songs based on similar criteria. A quick internet search will bring up the top songs across years and within genres.

The criteria could be:

1. Order of sections

2. Time-To-Chorus

3. Number of Verses

4. Number of Choruses

5. Number of non-Verse/Chorus sections (Bridges, Solos, breakdowns etc.)

6. How many songs have a Lead guitar solo

7. Overall duration of the song in minutes and seconds

Popular formats

The structure of a song is commonly referred to as a 'format'. The format is commonly written using letters to denote each section in the order it appears. The first section played will always be 'A' and this could be a Verse, Chorus, Solo or other section. Some formats don't specifically have Verses and Choruses. For example, the AABA format of 'Yesterday', by The Beatles, starts with the Hook which is repeated twice (AA), then followed by a Bridge (B). Section A then repeats until the end of the song. A common popular format is to start with a Verse, followed by a Chorus. The Verse/Chorus combination is repeated and followed by a Solo or Bridge as a means to add contrast to the pattern. This often returns to a repeating Chorus Outro. The complete format for this song would be ABABCBB. Let's look a little closer at this format below.

Common pop music format: ABABCB

Where 'A' is the Verse, 'B' is the Chorus, and 'C' is the Bridge
To expand: Verse 1/Chorus 1/Verse 2/Chorus 2/Bridge/Chorus 3

In this example, the Verse plays twice, while the Chorus plays three times. Each section might commonly play for an 8 bar sequence. It's quite common to repeat the final Chorus if the song has a fade, resulting in ABABCBB. The fourth Chorus may also be added so that it can be embellished with additional elements like free-style 'ad-lib' vocals or Lead guitar solos. This 'riffing' helps add variety to a highly repetitive Chorus. Finishing the song with two Choruses is intended to create impact and a lasting impression for the listener.

The frequency, repetition, and placement of sections, is critical in achieving and maintaining listener enjoyment

There are other variations on this basic format. For example this basic structure can be embellished by additional short Bridge sections between a Verse and Chorus. In this case, the structure might be shown like this:

ABCABCDC (Verse 1, Bridge 1, Chorus 1, Verse 2, Bridge 2, Chorus 2, Middle-8, Chorus 3)

Note: The term 'Bridge' can be confusing as it's commonly used synonymously with 'Middle-8'. Both of these terms refer to a musical section used later in a song to add contrast and break up the repetitive pattern of the song. In this example, it is used for its other meaning; to create a short transitionary section to join a Verse and Chorus section.

Other formats with song examples

AAAA (each repeating section includes the Hook)
Maggie May – Rod Steward
Bridge Over Troubled Water – Simon and Garfunkel

AABA (the Hook is in A)
Ain't No Sunshine – Bill Withers
I'll Never Fall in Love Again – Burt Bacharach
Just The Way You Are – Billy Joel

ABAB (the Chorus/Hook is in B)
Material Girl – Madonna
Somebody That I Used To Know – Gotye ft. Kimbra
Every Little Thing She Does Is Magic – The Police

ABA
Hotel California – The Eagles
Back in Black – ACDC

Radio wants what radio needs

Over the decades radio audiences have become conditioned to expect specific styles of arrangements common in popular music because of the way radio consistently delivers set-format radio hits. A song's format can have a major effect on the saleability and listenability of a song played on mainstream radio.

If the song release is planned for main-stream radio, a fairly limited range of formats is almost dictated because of things like song duration, TTC (Time-To-Chorus), and strength of the Hook. Your 11 minute long epic, as rich and colourful that it is, will unlikely get airplay on main-stream radio. Conversely, a musical composition intended for alternative or B-net ratio stations can have a lot more freedom to its structure. For instance, if the station plays mainly Indie music, there would likely be more latitude in the styles of format accepted.

The key point is to know your audience and the destination of your song. Are these songs for teens or mature audiences? Male or female? Radio or film? What genre are you aiming for? All of these elements need careful consideration if you want the music to reach its intended destination.

Stylistic differences between musical genres are greatly affected by the structure

Using a common format can help your song fit within a musical genre simply by maintaining a familiar structure. For example, an ABCD structure could work well if you're going for a long and meandering 13 minute arrangement in the same way that sticking with the ABABCBB format will help your song stay in the pop and rock genre. At the same time, a unique and unexpected style can be created within an existing genre by using an unlikely arrangement.

If you're not aiming for radio-play with your songs, then trying out alternative options with song structure can be rewarding. You may come up with something that gives a signature sound to your music. If nothing else, it can be a lot of fun messing around!

Application

1. Write down the format for each song
Writing down the format enables you to see potential problems and opportunities with the song's structure, like sequence problems and excessive repetition of sections.

2. Think of the Verse as a 'tension creator'
Verses in a song generate tension for the listener by creating anticipation for the Hook or Chorus. Conversely, Verses provide the listener with a reprieve from the Hook/Chorus, helping to alleviate the boredom created by 'over-cooking' the Hook. Use the Verses carefully so that they fulfil their function.

3. Think of the Chorus or Hook as the 'release'
Much like sugary treats, Choruses and Hooks are wonderful to have but they're best taken infrequently. The Chorus/Hook is the party everyone's been waiting for and once they arrive, they should be worth the wait. Your main focus is about getting the Chorus/Hook to be as powerful, catchy and memorable as possible.

4. Think of the Bridge, Middle-8 or Solo section as a 'refresher'
This section is a bit like eating sorbet after your restaurant main course. After two or three cycles of the Verse/Chorus, the listener needs to have their palate cleansed before launching them back into the Chorus/Hook.

5. Analyse the formats of popular songs
Look for similarities in the sequence and repetition of song sections in popular music. This is an effective way to improve your own work by emulating the formats used by the professionals.

6

Dynamics

The song's energy dynamic is affected by the arrangement and performance of sections, resulting in an ever-changing intensity of energy as the song progresses

A song can be considered as a sequence of sections with a contrasting, dynamic flow of energy

Each section in a song sequence can be manipulated to change the energy intensity. When your song has a varying intensity of energy, you create variation and therefore, an interesting listening experience for your audience. We might design our song to have low energy intensity in the first Verse then abruptly change to much higher energy in the Choruses. Subsequent Verses may be increased so that each one has more intensity than the last, yet still allowing a big step up to the Chorus. The big question is how to create this in a song.

Let's consider a slow-tempo, emotionally charged, rock song about 'lost love'. The song starts with a low energy first Verse and an, 'I'm sad you left me' theme. This is achieved by sparse instrumentation and an element of misery by the Lead vocalist's delivery. The song quickly builds in intensity to a loud and angry, 'I hate you for cheating on me' themed Chorus. This increase in energy is achieved by the full band playing with intensity and the Lead singer belting out a very aggressive vocal delivery. The song then quickly drops back to a quiet interlude. This very dynamic Intro/Verse/Chorus pattern of sections is then repeated before moving into a medium energy Bridge/Solo. This is followed by a highly energetic Chorus/Outro with guitar solos and high-energy ad-libbing by the Lead vocalist.

Stepping back, we've created a song with huge energy variation between the sections. Our song is a roller-coaster ride of musical and emotional energy that matches the song's theme perfectly.

Creating and using a Dynamics Map is essential in the arrangement process

A Dynamics Map is a simple tool that allows you to graphically describe the energy dynamics of all sections in a song. The map shows the relationship between song sections and provides a simple and powerful guide in helping sculpt the energy intensity of sections by showing Hooks, Builds, and Transitions.

It directly relates to the song's format and lyric sheet and it's quick and easy to make and revise. It's also a great tool for explaining your intentions about performance and song energy dynamics with others involved.

The Dynamics Map includes all song sections in order, along the x axis. The width of each block approximates the duration of each section. The Y axis approximates the dynamic (changing) energy level, from silence (base line) to low, medium and high. Drawing in the blocks is fairly self-explanatory from the image.

Don't get hung up on perfection when drawing your Dynamics Map. The point is to create a quick and simple graphic that shows the approximate energy level for each section. It's important to get the map done early on so you can discuss your intentions about the performance with the artist or band.

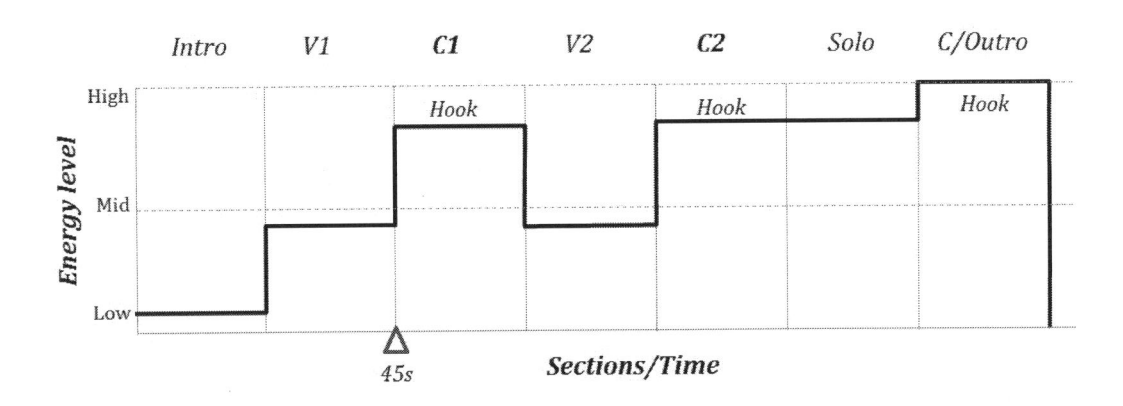

Image A: Dynamics Map for a Simple Pop Song
This example shows a song in ABABCB format. The song Intro starts with very low energy intensity, comprising a solo acoustic guitar. In Verse 1 the graph shows the energy dynamic stepping up significantly to medium. This equates to adding drums, bass and Lead vocals to the acoustic guitar. The entire band plays at average intensity. At Chorus 1, the energy steps up to high by adding electric guitars, keyboards and backing vocals. Other elements of the performance contribute to the energy increase. These include a loud and emotional delivery by the Lead vocalist and the drummer hitting harder with more liberal use of cymbals. Verse 2 sees the song energy settling back down significantly, but still at a higher level than Verse 1. The song steps up again to Chorus 2, with an equal energy to Chorus 1. This is followed by a high energy Solo, then a Chorus/Outro with an even higher energy level.

The energy of any section can be affected by volume, tempo, complexity, and emotion

In the above Dynamics Map example, it's difficult to understand what is actually meant by low, medium, and high energy. How is this actually achieved and how does the arrangement process control this for best effect? The energy of any section can be affected by volume, tempo, complexity, and emotion. Including all four of these components can result in a very high energy or intense performance; perfect for our rock Chorus. Limiting these components reduces the energy; perfect for our Verse.

Let's look at an example of a high energy Chorus that incorporates volume, tempo, complexity and emotion:

Drums:
Hit harder (volume increase), more drums and cymbals played than in the previous Verse (more complexity)

Lead vocals:
Sung louder (volume increase), sung with high intensity and anger (emotional)

More instruments playing: (added guitars, keyboards and backing vocals) More elements (volume increase) more different phrasing and added 'colour' from different sounds (more complexity).

Propensity for intensity

It's useful to note that some musical elements can deliver intensity far more obviously than others. For example, a Lead vocalist can create a much more obvious energy increase than a bass player. Similarly, a drummer can add massive energy by hitting harder and playing more complex rhythms.

The importance for the arranger is to know which musical elements and methods are best for manipulating energy intensity in the song sections.

The manipulation of a song's energy dynamic is a critical part of any song arrangement

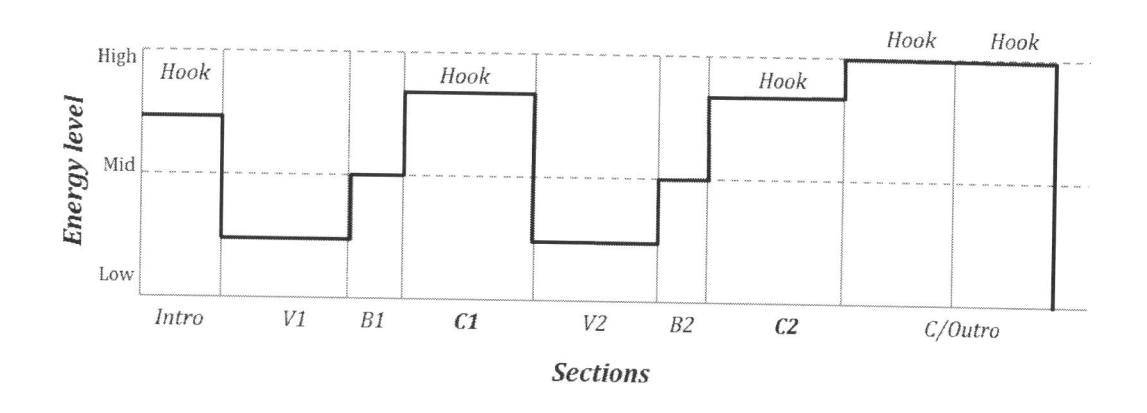

[Energy level graph showing sections: Intro, V1, B1, C1, V2, B2, C2, C/Outro — with Hooks marked on Intro, C1, C2, and C/Outro]

Image B: Dynamics Map – Alternative Structure A

Starting a song on a high can be a great way to get listener attention, especially if it includes a strong Hook. The sharp contrast in intensity between the Intro and the Verse creates further impact for the listener. The song progresses from the low energy Verse 1 into a short Bridge where the energy intensity is increased before moving into the Chorus. A pattern is quite visible here where the energy increase is much gentler between the Verse and Chorus, yet quite severe when moving from the Chorus to the Verse.

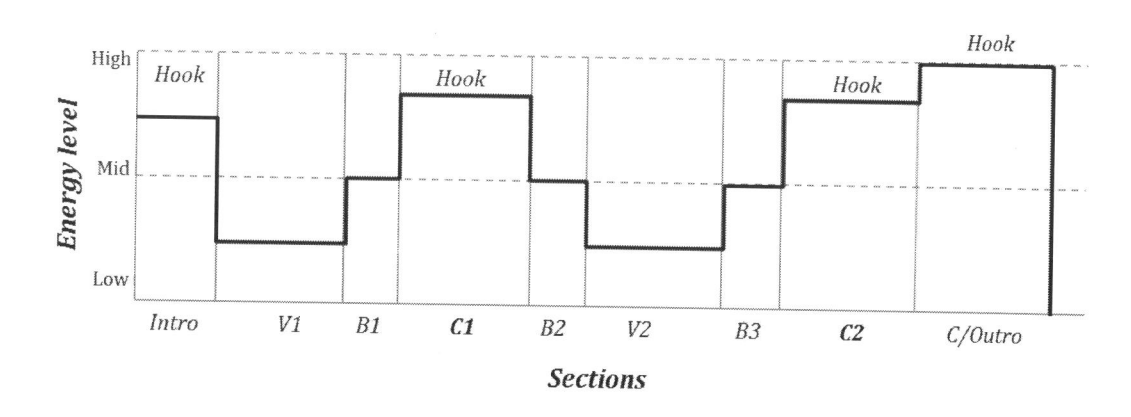

[Energy level graph showing sections: Intro, V1, B1, C1, B2, V2, B3, C2, C/Outro — with Hooks marked on Intro, C1, C2, and C/Outro]

Image C: Dynamics Map - Alternative Structure B

This song has a more fluid flow of energy between sections. Each section has a short Bridge section (B1, B2, B3) played between the Verse and Chorus that helps the progression from Verse to Chorus. The big dynamic drop from Chorus to Verse is absent as in Image A.

Application

1. Create a Dynamics Map for every song
A Dynamics Map provides a useful graphical representation of the flow of energy intensity in a song. It's useful when discussing the arrangement with musicians, engineers and producers because it makes a complex topic quick and easy to understand. You can find a blank one at the end of this book in the Checklist chapter.

2. Look at ways to create contrast between sections
The Dynamics Map makes it easy to visualise the contrast between sections. You can create significant contrast by huge energy drops and rises or you can have a more gradual flow between sections by using Transitions (more about Transitions in the next chapter).

3. Manipulate intensity by using volume, tempo, complexity, and emotion
When designing the energy intensity of song sections, start thinking about how combinations and interactions of musical elements contribute to create that energy.

4. Analyse the dynamic flow of popular songs
Create Dynamics Maps of popular songs and get an insight into how the professionals arrange their music. Look for patterns in different genres. You can reproduce these patterns and dynamic flow into your own songs.

7

Transitions

A Transition is a variation in the musical composition used to signal the progression from one musical section to the next

A Transition is an effective way to cue the listener about the upcoming section in a song

A musical Transition is an effective way to subtly alert the listener to a change between sections in a song. A song typically has many Transitions, with each being located in approximately the last bar or two of a section. A typical location is at the end of a Verse leading into a Chorus.

Transitions can be subtle or obvious depending on the listening experience you want to create. A subtle example is when moving from a Verse to a Chorus, the guitarist changes from playing a 'tight' rhythm phrasing to strummed and sustained chords in the last bar. An obvious Transition could be a drum fill or guitar solo.

The duration and style of the Transition can be done purely to taste, but it needs to be sympathetic with the song. Adding Transitions at the end of song sections is one simple tool that can really add a professional touch to any song arrangement.

There are endless ways that Transitions can be created. The important point is to make a conscious decision to either use them or not. The next important point is how they are crafted for maximum impact for the listener. Even the absence of a Transition can create quite a dramatic listening experience, such as moving from a quietly played Verse to an 'all guns blazing' Chorus. A careful approach to arrangement would have you making careful choices about how the song transitions from one section to another.

Use a Dynamics Map to help you map out the Transitions in a song

Planning and annotating your Transitions on a Dynamics Map is an effective way to capture and show how the Transitions might be created and where they would occur in the song. Showing Transitions graphically is very helpful in expressing your ideas to all the other folks involved in the song process.

Transitions are constructed by musical elements, effects or production techniques

Looking in more detail, a Transition is a change in the composition of musical elements at the end of a musical section. They can be a change in performance of the existing instruments, the introduction of new elements, or a combination of both. They can also be created by production techniques and effects. There are no hard-and-fast rules about what a Transition should sound like. Importantly, Transitions can be constructed and performed during recording, and created during the mixing process.

Transitions can be very effective when used subtly – resist the urge to 'smack the listener in the face' with every Transition. What's most important is that the style and pace of the Transition should be sympathetic with the overall song. A simple and 'safe' approach to creating a Transition is to use an existing musical element in the song and have it played differently for the Transition period.

15 Examples of Transitions

Here are simple and complex examples of how a Transition might be created in the last bar of a Verse leading to a Chorus on a typical rock song. Generally, the duration of a Transition works well over one to two bars.

1. A drum fill is played in combination with all other musical elements.
2. All musical elements stop and a drum fill is played.
3. Drums effected with band-limited 'AM radio' style effect.
4. Entire drum kit rendered, reversed, and mixed back into the main drum kit.
5. An electric guitar Transitions from a short staccato style to a series of sustained chords.
6. Reversed stereo electric guitars faded in to the end of the section.
7. The electric bass is muted.
8. All instruments play a series of punctuated stabs.
9. A keyboard with a volume swell builds over the duration of the bar.
10. All instrumentation in the song except the drums is reversed (played backwards).
11. Backing vocals are added to the main vocal.
12. The Lead vocal has a radio effect placed on the last phrase in that bar.
13. A stutter effect is created by 'chopping' or muting the entire song.
14. Arpeggio keyboard part.
15. Everything is muted for half a bar.

Carefully located, the purposeful absence of a Transition can create huge impact for the listener

The absence of a Transition can be a powerful tool

While using Transitions is incredibly effective in helping the song progress for listeners, not using Transitions can create massive impact between highly contrasting sections. For instance, consider a song with a low energy Verse and high energy Chorus. We already know that a Transition at the Verse/Chorus change-over prepares the listener for the big energy jump in the Chorus. However, not using a Transition can create huge impact by surprising the listener. This approach works just as well when moving from high energy down to low energy song sections.

It stands to reason that if there is minimal difference in energy between two adjoining sections, then the 'no Transition' approach is of little value. In this case, using Transitions is far more useful.

During the arrangement process, it's important to be aware of the progression between song sections, and be purposeful about the treatment you apply.

Tricking our listeners with Transitions

It's fairly clear by now that Transitions are an effective way to cue our listener to an increase or decrease in energy in the upcoming section. But what if we cue them for something big, then progress to something small? And what if the energy difference is huge between the two sections? This is another great method to create impact by fooling the listener; we prepare them for one thing, and then do something completely unexpected.

Perhaps a perfect example of this is at a Chorus/Solo position in a song. Let's say our song has a high energy Chorus and we want the listener to think we are transitioning into a high energy, face-melting guitar solo. We cue the listener with a Transition 'ramp up', and lead into...an extremely gently played solo over a softly-played instrumentation.

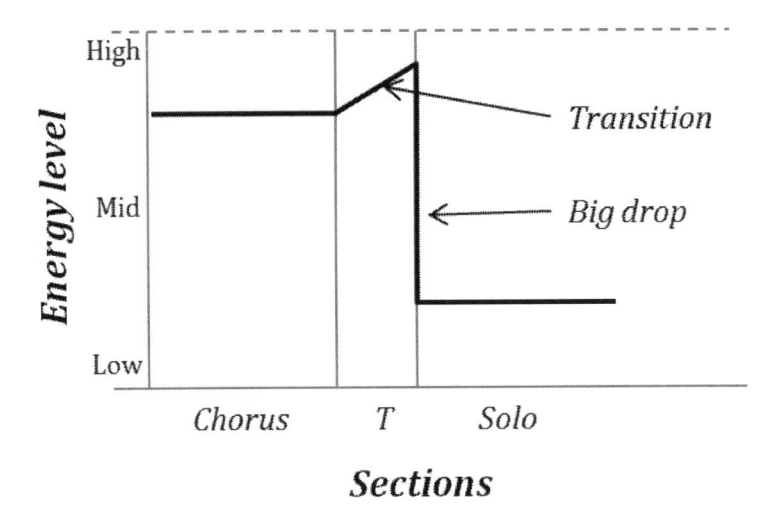

Image D: The 'Cliff-hanger' Transition
This example shows a huge contrast between a Chorus and a Solo, where the listener is cued for an energy increase, but the opposite occurs.

These types of high-impact techniques can have quite a jarring effect for listeners, so it's important to use them with care. Clearly, they're not always appropriate for every song. Also, the impact of these methods can be lost if they are over-used in a song.

Even the most subtle use of Transitions can transform the quality of a song recording

Transitions don't need to be slap-in-the-face-obvious to be effective. In many cases they can be a subtle variation or the addition of one or two simple elements. The important point is that they add something different or new just before the next song section. Even at a very subtle level, they cue the listener into the next section, preparing and guiding them, and helping to create a satisfying listening experience.

Application

1. Apply Transitions in your songs
Start thinking about Transitions as a method to cue your listener into and out of a song section. Keep your Transitions short; around one bar duration usually works but it's completely up to you. You can also create great contrast in a song by establishing interesting Transition patterns. For example, in a song you might transition only from Verses to Choruses and use no Transitions at the end of Choruses. This pattern could create a gentle energy rise into a Chorus and a big dynamic drop out of the Chorus if the Verse is musically sparse. Refer to image B above for an example of this.

2. Use a Dynamics Map to plan your Transitions
The Dynamics Map is a great way to show a visual representation of all the Transitions in a song. It's a great way to see, at a glance, how Transitions can work across an entire song. It's also very helpful in explaining your ideas to others in the song production process.

3. Create Transitions using a range of techniques
You can create incredible variety in your Transitions by using existing musical elements, production techniques and effects. Refer to the 15 previous examples for some ideas about how to achieve this.

4. Experiment with subtle and distinct Transitions
Try and avoid the 'smack-in-the-face' approach when creating Transitions. Subtle Transitions like those stated above can add incredible professionalism to your arrangements.

5. Plan your Transitions for the performance and the mixing stage
Planning a song's Transitions early will help you differentiate what is done during recording and what is done during mixing.

6. Analyse existing songs
There are many great examples of the use of Transitions in popular music. An effective way to get ideas is to listen to how Transitions have been created in these songs. You might be surprised at how simple and effective these can be.

8 Builds

The addition of musical elements to add variation and energy to repeating song sections

A Build is a simple and effective way to add variation to a repeated musical section

The repeating of musical sections in a song is an important method for building listener familiarity with the song. However, a lack of variation from over-repetition of sections can be very boring and 'one dimensional' for listeners. A Build typically introduces new elements while retaining the basic characteristics of the original section. The point of a Build is not to drastically change the repeated section, but to add variation and a change in the energy intensity. Builds are typically applied to Verses and Choruses as these are the most often repeated sections. In contrast to Transitions, Builds add new musical content that usually occur over the full duration of that section.

Builds can be created in a variety of ways

Builds can be created in a number of different ways, such as:

1. A more intense performance
Example: A louder or more emotionally charged Lead vocal is a typical example.

2. A more complex performance
Examples: A vocalist delivering more lyrics in the same time duration, a vocalist using more complex melody or phrasing, a drummer playing more drums/cymbals or varied time signatures.

3. A faster performance (tempo)
Examples: The tempo of a section increases, such as having faster Choruses and slower Verses. The song's tempo remains consistent but the instrument of vocal plays more quickly, like a bass player moving from playing 1/4 notes to 1/8 notes or a vocalist singing more quickly.

4. The addition of new musical instrumentation and vocals
Example: The addition of backing vocals to support a Lead vocal, the addition of guitars to support existing guitar (like adding a Lead to a rhythm), adding an organ to add 'thickness' and sustain.

5. The addition of production elements like loops and samples
Example: Third-party production samples, samples of the song (such as a 1 bar reversed loop), single drum hits, orchestra stabs, anything you can possibly imagine.

6. The use of effects on existing musical elements

Example: 'AM Radio' effects on vocals, Chorus, delay, reverb, and specialist plugins (like Izotope's Stutter Edit and Breaktweaker instrument plugins).

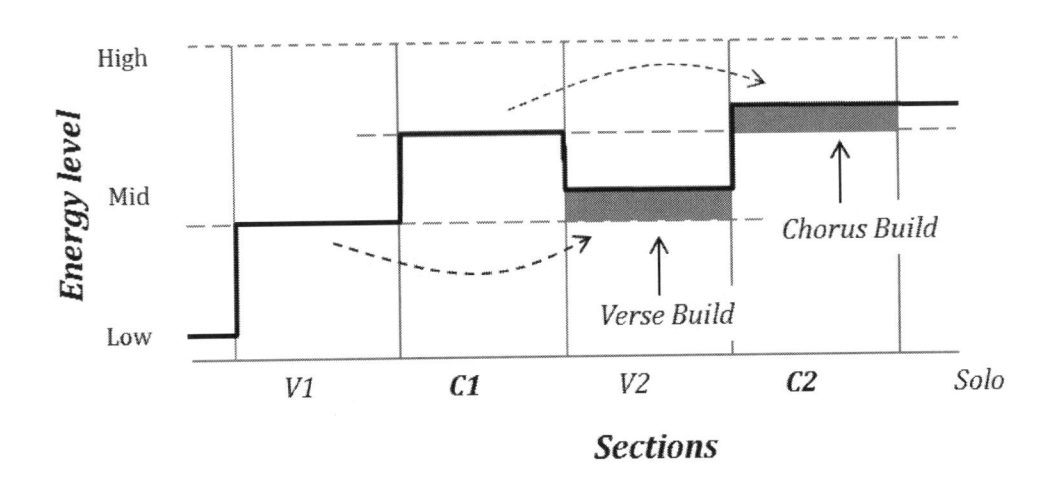

Image E: Energy Build Between Song Sections
This image shows a typical energy Build between two Verses and two Choruses, indicated by the grey shaded area. Verse 2 has an increase in energy over Verse 1. Similarly, Chorus 2 has an increase over the first Chorus.

Creating Builds by addition

A simple way to Build a song section is to increase the number of elements playing. For instance, adding a Lead guitar to a section with an existing rhythm guitar can work. If the goal is to create a very obvious build, then the new element should have different tonal and performance characteristics. Conversely, if the goal is to create a subtle Build, the new guitar would sound more similar to the existing; perhaps it plays a different rhythm using a different pickup selection.

Another approach is to add a different instrument with a very different sound. In rock music, the addition of an organ to a drum/bass/guitar combo is a classic example. In addition to the new tonal colour, organ has a powerful sustain character that will give a thickening effect to the overall sound.

This method is one that can be created in both the recording and the mixing phase of the production. Assuming that extra tracks have been recorded in the first place, it's simply a case of including these in the final mix. As an example, it might be the case of having one guitar panned left in Verse 1, then adding another, panned right, in the second Verse.

Creating Builds using performance intensity

Using performance intensity is a great way to Build a section without actually adding any new musical elements. It's important to be able to recognise what intensity sounds like and how to achieve it across a range of musical elements. Most importantly, the capture of the desired performance needs to happen during the recording phase – it's not something that is recreated during mixing using effects and plugins. To prepare for this requires careful listening to the band's performance before recording. It's important to discuss each member's performance for each song section so that the desired level of intensity is achieved.

Let's consider the example of a vocalist in a rock band. Our objective is to craft her performance intensity for the entire song. We want all Choruses to have a consistently high intensity. Also, the Verses need to be at a much lower intensity so that obvious contrast is created between Verses and Choruses. In the Chorus/Outro, we want to finish the song on an even higher intensity.

Our discussion with the vocalist would be about using volume and emotion in the Choruses; in other words, singing loudly with passion. We're not necessarily asking her to sing faster (quicker phrasing).
Using a Dynamics Map would make it much easier to describe our intentions to the vocalist. This also creates a useful visual guide for the entire band during rehearsal and recording.

If you Build too fast you can peak too early

Try and avoid Building your song sections too early. This can make it difficult to create an overall progression where each Build is bigger than the previous one. For example, if your song has three Verses, you would avoid creating a big Build in Verse 2, as you still want to leave 'room' to add new elements for the next Build in Verse 3. This principle of 'pacing' the Builds applies to all sections in the song.

Incorporating Builds is an effective way to add variation and energy to a repetitive song structure

There are times in a song when a Build on a third Verse just doesn't work. This is usually because the previous verse seems to have reached maximum perceived energy. This may be because we don't want it to add further intensity, complexity, or volume. A well-used technique in this situation is to strip the music right back to the bare essentials on the third iteration. This drastic change creates considerable contrast, effectively achieving the goal: to create variation by a change in intensity.

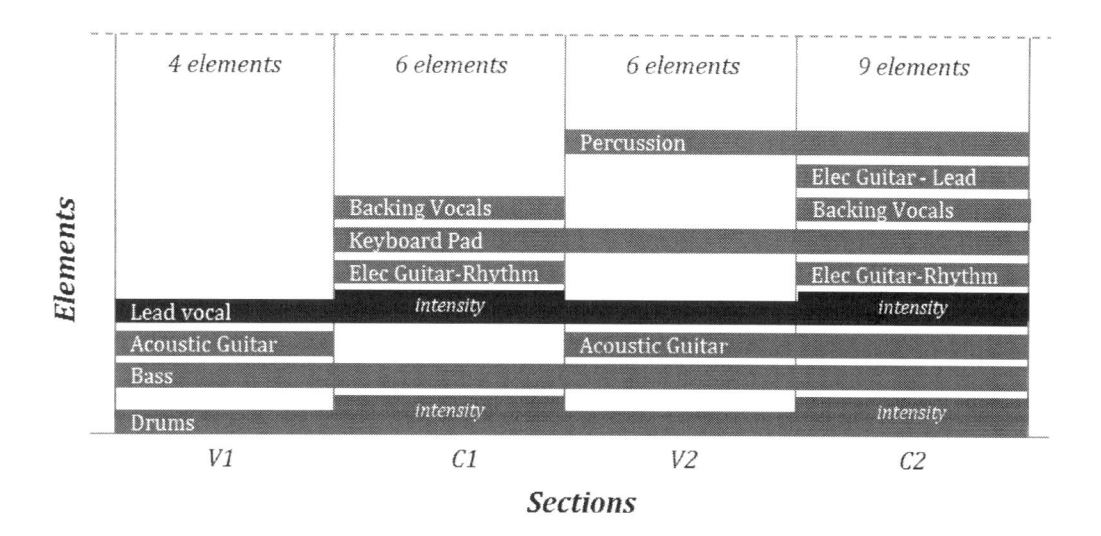

Elements	V1 (4 elements)	C1 (6 elements)	V2 (6 elements)	C2 (9 elements)
			Percussion	Elec Guitar - Lead
		Backing Vocals		Backing Vocals
		Keyboard Pad		
		Elec Guitar-Rhythm		Elec Guitar-Rhythm
	Lead vocal	intensity		intensity
	Acoustic Guitar		Acoustic Guitar	
	Bass			
	Drums	intensity		intensity

Sections

Image F: Creating 'Builds' Using Addition And Intensity
This shows how the number of musical elements and their intensity can be used to create Builds in a song. The thicker grey bars indicate a more intense performance of an element. For example, a Lead vocal could deliver more intensity (emotion and volume) in Choruses to create the necessary Builds in those sections.

Santa Monica by Everclear

This song has very obvious Builds from section to section, where new elements are systematically introduced in a very linear fashion. The song starts with a guitar only, quickly adding a Lead vocal then a bass and hi-hat. Before the Verse gets to the Chorus the full band is playing. However, the song energy drops into a short interlude after the first Chorus, then takes a leap in energy into the second Verse. This is demonstrated by a more intense drum beat and energetic guitar playing. From there, the song builds higher and higher. This is a very good example where Builds have been used very prominently to create a signature sound to this song.

Application

1. Use Builds to add interest and variation
This is a powerful technique for adding a professional touch to a song arrangement. Start focusing on how you can add variation and interest to the different sections in a song.

2. Create your Builds using intensity, complexity, tempo and addition
Each of these methods can be used individually or in combination to Build the sections in your song.

3. Don't peak too early
When Builds are created by adding more musical elements, the energy dynamic of the song can be raised to quickly causing the song to 'peak' too early. For example, if your song has three Verses and you peak in the second Verse you may find it difficult to Build in the third. Similarly, Building the Verses too much may mean the Chorus struggles to be the climax of the song.

4. Plan your Builds for the performance and the mixing stage
Decide early on which Builds will be created by the performance and which will be done by adding new elements. Builds using intensity, like an emotional Lead vocal, must be captured in the recording stage; they can't be created using effects. Builds that simply require the addition of a new element can often easily be done by adding or re-amping existing recorded tracks.

5. Show your builds on a Dynamics Map
The Dynamics Map is a great way to show a visual representation of Builds across an entire song. A big benefit is the way that the entire song can be seen, showing the relationship of Builds across different sections. It's also very useful when discussing with others because the graphical nature communicates this very easily.

6. Analyse the Builds in popular music
Check out popular songs and make a note of how Builds are used in the song's sections. Again, this is a good technique for making your own library of ideas.

9

Groove

The interaction of drums, bass and rhythmical elements in a song

The groove is the interaction of foundation and rhythmical components that give a song momentum and vibe

A strong groove is often the signature sound of musical genres such as hip-hop, disco and funk. A groove is fundamentally created by the interaction between the drums and bass, and enhanced by rhythm components such as guitar, keyboards, and horns. So infectious are these drum and bass grooves, that they are often an integral part of the song, irrespective of a strong vocal melody.

A strong groove can turn an otherwise understated rhythm section into a prominent and powerful partnership. There are many great examples of this, such as James Brown's 'Sex Machine', and Tower of Power's 'Maybe it'll Rub Off'. In many cases, the bass lines are extremely catchy due to being so well phrased and heavily melodic, with the Police's, 'Walking On The Moon', and Queen's, 'Another One Bites The Dust', being perfect examples of this.

The groove can carry the song

There's nothing quite so compelling as a song that seems to grab you by the shirt and makes you want to get up and dance. In many cases, it is the interaction between a solid drum beat, a prominent bass line, and a punctuating rhythm element that creates such a compelling groove. Average White Band's song, 'Cut The Cake' is a perfect example of this drum, bass, and guitar combination. Check.

While the examples raised so far have focused on funk and disco, powerful drum/bass grooves are evident in songs across many genres; from Pink Floyd to Michael Jackson; from Rock to Pop. A major advantage of a strong groove in an arrangement is that, coupled with a strong Chorus Hook, it can make a song imminently more listenable than a song that relies on a Chorus Hook alone.

A collection of songs with great grooves from different genres:

Age of Reason – John Farnham

Another One Bites The Dust – Queen

Are you in? – Incubus

Billie Jean – Michael Jackson

Come Together – The Beatles

Cut the Cake – Average White Band

Fool's Gold – The Stone Roses

Get Up – James Brown

Give It Away Now – The Red Hot Chilli Peppers

Graceland – Paul Simon

Give Up The Funk - Parliament

Mustang Sally – The Commitments

Play That Funky Music – Wild Cherry

Shaky Ground – Phoebe Snow

Superfreak – Rick James

Superstition – Stevie Wonder

Uptown Funk – Mark Ronson ft Bruno Mars

Walking On the Moon – The Police

We Are Family – Sister Sledge

Stuck In The Middle With You – Stealers Wheel

Application

1. Improve the groove
Listen carefully to the way the bass player and drummer interact with each other. Also listen for supporting rhythmical elements such as guitars, keyboards and horns: how do these contribute? Can you improve the groove? Does it feel like groove elements are fighting or working in harmony? It may be that the bass playing is too complex or not locking in with the kick drum. Your role is to get the groove 'sitting right'. If the hairs stand up on your neck and you want to get up and dance then the groove is probably just right.

2. Create variation
Even a great groove can become boring when it's repeated continuously. Focus on how you might add subtle or distinct variation to the groove in different song sections, Transitions and Builds. Remember that this needs to be agreed with the band early on so that they can get their performance right for the recording.

3. Be aware of groove versus genre
In the same way that the funk genre is dominated by a rhythm section's groove, other musical styles have more or less emphasis on the groove. A particularly strong groove may be enough to change a song's genre or move it into a sub-genre. Does this fit with your audience expectations? Will your designated radio station play this?

4. The groove + Hook combination
Can you add value to your arrangement by having a great groove to accompany your song's Hook? Focusing on the groove and looking at ways to make it more prominent can add value to the arrangement.

5. Analyse existing popular songs
If you're not familiar with the effect that a strong groove can have on a song, listen to the song examples above and try and get a sense of how compelling a strong groove can be. There are many instances where a song's groove is so powerful it becomes the Hook. These examples cover pop, rock, funk, disco and country genres.

10

The Hook

The value of melodic phrasing and the importance of the Hook

Hooks can be rhythmic, melodic and instrumental

In modern popular music it's easy to think of a Hook as simply a catchy vocal melody residing in the Chorus. However, a song's Hook can be constructed in a variety of ways. It can be a compelling rhythmical groove, like in Stevie Wonder's 'Superstition', the Lead guitar Intro in Chris Rea's 'Down On The Beach', or the captivating vocal rap Chorus in Grandmaster Flash and the Furious Five's 'The Message'.

The Hook can take a different form in every song and part of the arrangement process is to identify the Hook, or Hooks, and 'work' them (more on 'working the Hook' later in this chapter).

Examples of Hooks in popular songs

Another One Bites The Dust – Queen
The initial Hook is created by the bass line and simple drum beat at the start of the song. The second Hook is the vocal phrase "Another one bites the dust".

Down on the Beach – Chris Rea
The initial Lead guitar phrase at the beginning of the song.

The Message – Grandmaster Flash and the Furious Five
The vocal phrase "It's like a jungle sometimes it makes me wonder how I keep from going under".

Wannabe – The Spice Girls
This song has a double Hook. The first being the lyrical rap phrase, "Tell me what you want, what you really, really want", which is well supported by the solid and punctuated riff created by the rhythm section. The second Hook is the Chorus lyrics, "If you wannabe my lover…". Incidentally, in 2014, researchers conducted a one year experiment called 'Hooked On Music' where 12,000 participants picked the Spice Girls' song 'Wannabe' as the most popular song from over 1,000 clips played from a 70 year period.

You Can Call Me Al – Paul Simon
This song has multiple Hooks. The first Hook is established at the beginning of the song by the interaction between the rhythm section and the horn section then repeated throughout. The vocal in the Chorus also creates a strong melodic Hook. Last but not least, this song has an incredibly compelling bass groove throughout.

<u>Walking on the Moon – The Police</u>
This is another example of a song with multiple Hooks. The first Hook occurs at the start of the song with the interaction between the bass and the rhythm guitar. The second Hook occurs in the vocal melody of the first section where the song title is repeated.

<u>My Sharona – The Knack</u>
This song starts with a powerful 'riffy' instrumental groove, with a second Hook in the Chorus vocals, "my, my, my-yi-yi, ooh…ma, ma, my sharona". The song also repeats the word "Sharona" regularly throughout the Verses, affectively reinstating the song title. This is a very catchy song with multiple Hooks from a combination of clever riffs and catchy vocal phrasing and melodies.

<u>We Will Rock You – Queen</u>
The song has two distinct Hooks. The first is the distinctive 'stomp-stomp-clap' rhythm and the second is vocal melody in the Chorus. This stomp-stomp-clap rhythm is so iconic that the song is recognisable within seconds of starting. The song is also characterised by its prominent change into the guitar Solo/Outro.

The success of a Hook is in its strength, placement and repetition

The Hook in a song is only as powerful as the supporting music, its location in the song, and how often it occurs. All of these things matter when crafting a great song because the Hook is what keeps listeners coming back for more. The simplest way to emphasise a Hook is by repetition because repeating it y makes it more memorable. However, a weak Hook that is repeated over and over is more likely to bore a listener.

The placement of the Hook is vital to any song. For instance, locating the Hook early gives listeners a taster and then creates anticipation while they wait for the next repetition. Finishing a song with multiple repetitions of the Hook is certainly one way to ensure listeners go away humming your tune. Getting the total number of Hook repetitions right is critical because 'over-cooking' can bore the listener, just as 'under-cooking' can leave the listener unsatisfied.

The Hook is the strongest and most memorable musical phrase in a song

Getting the Hook's repetition right is dictated by the song's structure and tempo, and therefore, varies from song to song. A slow tempo might take longer to get to the Chorus/Hook and you might alter the song structure to get to the Hook faster. This might mean shortening a Verse length or re-ordering the sections. Be aware that altering the arrangement can significantly affect the composition so discuss it's worthwhile discussing with the songwriter.

'Working the Hook' is an art

'Working the Hook' is about finding ways to embellish it and make it special by implementing the principles of strength, placement and repetition. Improving the Hook might be achieved by simplifying the melody line and repeating it more. Sometimes, the best way to strengthen the hook is to alter those musical elements around it. In this way, you can use a two-fold approach. The main thing to remember is that a song's Hook is the star of the show and it needs to be treated accordingly.

Ideas for 'working' a weak vocal Hook in a Chorus

1. Reducing, removing, or altering the tonal qualities of musical elements that are causing frequency masking. For example, a vocal Hook can be masked by a dense 'wall of guitars' in a rock song.

2. Removing melodic phrases that are competing with the vocal melody, like a guitar or keyboard Lead.

3. Altering the harmonic structure of supporting instruments; possibly the hardest approach because it means changing the song and coming up with something better that the composer agrees with. This could mean altering the chord progression of instruments while maintaining the same vocal melody.

4. Adding supporting Lead elements that duplicate and reinforce the melody, such as backing vocals, a keyboard or a Lead guitar. Audioslave's song, 'Like A Stone' has a very nice example of this in the Verses where the Lead electric guitar plays a supporting melody in half-time to the Lead vocal (this is a good example even though it doesn't relate to a Chorus Hook).

5. Reducing the energy of the preceding Verse so that the song's perceived energy steps up from the Verse to the Chorus.

6. Using repetition to reinforce the Hook. Depending on the length of the phrase, up to four repeats can work well.

7. Reconstructing the Hook. This can be tough if you're not the songwriter because it means a discussion about changing somebody's masterpiece. However, done with integrity it can be rewarding for all involved. Sometimes it's the only option.

It could be argued that decades of radio hit format songs have conditioned listeners' expectations of where the Hook in a song should be. This can translate to an audience expecting that every song builds to a Chorus with a prominent Hook. If you're not sure about this, try arranging a song in a radio hit format where the Hook is in every Verse without a hint in the Chorus. Two things might become obvious. Firstly, the Hook becomes 'overcooked' and the Choruses lack magic and don't make sense. The song is confusing and listeners won't make sense of it. Getting the Hook right can make or break a song.

Songs with multiple Hooks can be incredibly engaging for listeners

Multiple Hooks result in multiple catchy elements in a song, providing more reasons for our listeners to want to listen again and again. Paul Simon's, 'You Can Call Me Al' is a great example where a bass-dominated rhythm, a memorable horn section, and a great vocal Chorus Hook combine to enthrall listeners.

Another great example is 'Walk This Way' by Aerosmith and Run DMC, where a strong Lead guitar Hook at the Intro is coupled with a strong vocal Hook in the Chorus. Many listeners would recognise these songs within seconds of starting due to their prominent Hooks.

The concept of multiple Hooks is simply that a song can have more than one. It then becomes important to identify what and where these are in a composition and focus on getting the strength, placement and repetition right by 'working the Hooks'.

Do you have a Hook-less song?

There are times when a song seems to lack a substantial Hook. Sometimes, in agreement with the songwriter, the best approach is to look for existing elements to strengthen rather than generating something entirely new.

A simple approach to identifying and creating Hooks is to consider them in terms of:

1. Vocal (melody and rhythm e.g. rapping)

2. Instrument melody (e.g. a horn phrase, a Lead guitar solo, a keyboard part)

3. Rhythm (e.g. a bass line, drum beat or combination of both)

Application

1. Learn to identify and 'work the Hook'
Learn to identify and 'work the Hook' to make it special. This may require you to work with the song-writer to improve it.

2. Use multiple Hooks
Learn to recognise Hooks in the variety of forms they take and be open to the possibility that your song may have more than one Hook. It's not uncommon for a song to have a groove Hook (from the rhythm section) and a melodic vocal Hook in a Chorus.

3. Focus on strength, placement and repetition
A certain amount of gut feel is required in how often a Hook should occur. A general guide is to locate the Hook in every Chorus, however, some AAA song formats start with the Hook. Whatever format you use, try and arrive at the Hook quickly. As a general rule, try and get there in around 30 to 45 seconds or less. Using a Dynamics Map is a great way to visualise the placement and repetition of the Hook.

4. Don't 'overcook' or 'undercook' the Hook
Avoid overusing the Hook because you don't want to bore your listeners. Also avoid under-use, which can leave a listener feeling unsatisfied.

5. Analyse the Hooks in popular songs
Analysing the Hooks in popular songs will show similarities in strength, placement and repetition. Look for common patterns around placement and repetition and compare these across a range of songs. Consider how you can use the same patterns in your own songs.

Here are some aspects to look at when analysing and comparing songs :
a) How long does it take to get to the Hook?
b) How many times is the Hook repeated?
c) In what sections does the Hook occur?
d) What is the actual time interval from Hook to Hook?
e) What similarities are evident when comparing the Hooks in different songs?

6. Resources
Check out **www.Hooktheory.com** where the author presents an interesting and revealing analysis of the Hooks of 1300 popular songs.

11

Tempo and duration

The pace and length of a song and how it affects song listenability

The pace of a song is affected by tempo, performance and structure

Selecting the best tempo for a song is usually done during composition but can often be altered during the arrangement. The goal is to get the song's pace 'feeling' right and pace is very much about perception. The pace of a song is affected by tempo, performance and structure. Suffice to say, adjustments in any of these three areas are very effective for fine-tuning the song's pace. For instance, a song of 100 BPM may feel like it 'drags' if the Lead vocalist is singing behind the time. Alternatively, the same song may have a faster pace if the drummer plays 16th notes on the hi-hat or the bass plays an 8th or 16th note bass line. Another way to increase the pace could be to alter the structure so the Chorus arrives more quickly; a song can certainly drag if there are too many Verses before the first Chorus occurs.

When a song's pace feels like its dragging, a tempo adjustment will seem like the obvious solution. However, this is not practical if the arrangement is being fine-tuned late in the recording stage. Also, adjusting the tempo won't always work if the pace issues are caused by performance of other instruments or a poor song structure. Any adjustments to a song's pace require a holistic consideration of tempo, performance and structure before changes are made.

Performance of vocals and instrumentation in the song can affect the perception of pace. A rhythm section may have a well-paced groove but the Lead vocal performance may seem hurried or dragging due to the phrasing and delivery. Similarly, a key guitar riff or bass line may feel uncomfortable if their phrasing and speed isn't sympathetic with the rest of the band. This may require a rework of guitar riffs, bass lines or lyrics to achieve a cohesive vibe where all the musical elements gel and flow at the chosen tempo.

Take the time to compare your song with the competition

If your song is destined to compete with others in a comparative genre then it's useful to compare the tempo and pace of your song with the competition. For example, at the time of writing this, many popular country music songs are sitting around the 130 BPM range. However, if you're involved in the arrangement of songs in the Country genre, use common tempos as a guide only and adjust the tempos according to the performance and structure.

Selecting a tempo that complements the song is critical in terms of getting the 'pace' of the song right

BPM (beats per minute) examples in modern Country genre:

This Is How We Roll - Florida Georgia Line - 132 bpm
You Belong To Me - Taylor Swift – 130 bpm
Perfect Day - Lady Antebellum – 128 bpm

It is typical for musical genres to fall into common tempo ranges. There's surely debate around an ideal song tempo for any genre, however, historical and current practice show similarities in each genre. It was common for Disco to have a tempo of around 120 BPM while other genres have their own characteristic tempo ranges. Even though there is a relationship between genre and tempo there are still obviously exclusions where slower or faster tempos occur.

BPM examples of Disco genre:

Last Dance – Donna Summer – 125 bpm
Good Times – Chic – 116 bpm
Disco Inferno – Tramps – 132 bpm
YMCA – Village People – 129 bpm
I Love The Nightlife – Alicia Bridges – 125 bpm

Tempo affects the duration of sections and the total length of the song

When songs have a slower tempo it takes longer to progress through each section and increases the total duration of the song. Depending on the length of each section this can affect how long the audience waits to get to the Chorus/Hook. For slower tempos in popular music it can be useful to have fewer or shorter sections between each Hook to reduce listener waiting time between Hooks. The slower tempo can also lead to the overall song being of longer duration if too many sections occur. Comparatively, faster tempos will speed up the movement through the sections potentially resulting in reaching the Hook too soon and too often. A faster tempo also gets a song more quickly to the finish.

Being aware of the impact of tempo on the song duration allows us to structure the length of sections, keep the song interesting and get the total duration right. The right tempo enables a song to get to the Chorus on time and spend the right amount of time there before moving on.

For some songs and genres the impact of tempo on the TTC (Time-To-Chorus) and the overall duration may not be an issue. However, if your song is destined for radio you may be aiming for TTC of 30 – 45 seconds, while also limiting the total song duration to around 3.30. To achieve this requires a careful arrangement of sections, their duration and song tempo.

Simple time analysis of popular songs

The following examples show the TTC and duration of popular songs and their similarities. Many radio hits have similar TTC's and duration but there are always the ones that buck the trend – see Mark Ronson's 'Uptown Funk' below.

Hot 'n' Cold: Katy Perry
Duration: 3.40
Time-To-Chorus: 32 seconds

Quarterback: Kira Isabella
2014, Top Ten Canadian billboard top 10
Duration: 3.30
Time-To-Chorus: 47 seconds

This is how we roll: Florida Georgia Line featuring Luke Bryan
2014 US No. 1 hit
Duration: 3.37
Time-To-Chorus: 36 seconds

She Looks So Perfect: 5 Seconds of Summer
Duration: 4:04
Time-To-Chorus: 45 seconds

Uptown Funk ft Bruno Mars: Mark Ronson
Duration: 4.31
Time-To-Chorus: 66 seconds

Wannabe: Spice Girls
Duration: 3.08
Time-To-Chorus: 40 seconds

Application

1. Song pace is affected by tempo, performance and song structure

Avoid having the song feel like it 'drags' or 'hurries'. Remember that the tempo is more than simply song BPM. The tempo interacts with the performance of all other elements and is affected by song structure. Listen carefully to the vocal primarily to ensure the delivery flows at what feels like a natural pace. Try listening to a recorded demo in your DAW and alter the tempo as needed.

2. Get the TTC right

Ensure your Time-To-Chorus is suitable for the intended audience. For radio airplay this often means getting to the Chorus within the first 30 seconds of the song. In the case of songs with an AAA format where the Chorus/Hook occurs at the start, the TTC for the next Chorus becomes important. This can mean altering the structure, such as removing a Verse or shortening excessively long Intro's.

3. Check the section and song duration

The song duration needs to suit the audience and the delivery format. For radio play this often requires a total duration of three to four minutes. A slower tempo may require shorter song sections or less of them to fall inside the ideal total song duration. For songs not intended for radio be mindful about maintaining enough variation to keep your listeners engaged; long meandering songs can be an artful delight or a complete bore!

4. Analyse popular songs

Check out songs in your genre for your audience and look at the similarities in terms of duration and TTC. If you want your songs to appeal to a particular audience then looking at commonalities related to time is important.

12

Establishing the Lead

Creating focus in a song by maintaining a strong Lead element

A strong Lead element commands listener attention

A song with a powerful Lead is engaging for listeners because it gives the song a strong focusing element, unhindered by competing musical elements. Rarely do we hear a song with two Lead vocals occurring simultaneously. Similarly, it's problematic to play drum fills with Lead vocals, or bass solos with guitar solos. There may be times in a song when dual Lead elements occur together, but ideally these occurrences would be short and done to make a statement.

The Primary Lead

The Lead can be constructed from a single element, such as a Lead vocal or a combination of elements that form one cohesive element. In popular music it's typical for the main - or Primary – Lead to be the main vocal. It's also common for the Primary lead to change, such as in a guitar solo or an instrumental Hook. In this example, the Primary Lead purposely alternates between a limited number of Lead elements. This variation helps keep the song sounding fresh, but all the time, the focus is on one Primary Lead at any one time.

Primary and Secondary Leads

A variation on this idea is to incorporate Secondary Lead elements; different musical elements with short phrasing that momentarily 'fill the holes' between the phrases of the Primary Lead. Typically, these are drum fills, guitar and keyboard riffs, and backing vocals. A very common example is where the Primary Lead is a main vocal punctuated by these short riffs at the end of the vocal phrases. An excellent example of this is the song 'Emotional Rescue' by The Rolling Stones.

A good arrangement would have an overall theme for constructing the Lead. Perhaps the song is dominated by a Primary Lead with Secondary Leads only introduced later in the song. Or maybe the aim is for a very intimate and emotionally charged song with one Primary Lead (main vocal) and no Secondary Leads. Whatever is decided in the arrangement requires deliberate intention so that the song is delivered with force and conviction, and holds the audience attention until the end.

Examples of Secondary Lead elements

+ Drum fills

+ Bass riffs

+ Lead guitar and Lead keyboard riffs

+ Keyboard pads

+ Backing vocals

+ Sound FX

+ Samples

A strong Lead can be created by careful selection and placement of elements throughout the song

In modern popular music the primary Lead is often the Lead vocal. However, when the Lead vocal is not being delivered (say in the pause at the end of a vocal phrase) another element can momentarily take the Lead. This creates an alternating pattern where the primary Lead (vocal) is replaced momentarily with a Secondary Lead at the end of each phrase.
Taking a holistic approach across an entire Verse or song, the arranger can develop and maintain consistency in the arrangement. This could mean that in the Verses these short Secondary Lead elements are perhaps a drum fill or a horn section phrase. Taking this approach is useful because it avoids using all sorts or random elements as Secondary Lead elements.

Manipulating the Leads can alter the energy as the song progresses

One way of developing the energy in a song is to reduce the Secondary Leads in earlier sections then increase them in later sections. This can be as simple as limiting the number of Secondary Leads in the first Verse and having more in the second. The same technique can be used with the Choruses. This approach allows the song's energy to 'build' as it progresses (see the chapter on Builds).

Another technique is to use 'warm' sounding Secondary Leads (sounds with limited high frequency content/transients) in early song sections. In later sections the song energy can be increased by choosing sounds with more transient energy and 'less warm' frequencies.

For example, a snare fill provides far more emphasis than "ooohs" from backing vocals. Similarly, a twangy electric guitar Lead riff grabs listener attention more than a warm bass fill.

A very common technique for creating a strong Lead emphasis in a Chorus is to have the guitarist playing short Lead riffs in the gaps between the Lead vocal lines. This provides a continuous focusing Lead element for listeners with no 'dead spots'.

Examples of songs with strong Lead emphasis

Monkey Wrench - The Foo Fighters
This highly energetic rock song is littered with short quarter-bar stops. In this example the introduction of silence is a huge contrast to the rest of the song and is extremely captivating for the listener.

Emotional Rescue - The Rolling Stones
This song exhibits a carefully constructed assortment of Lead elements.
In order from the start of the song are:

Intro: catchy bass riff in rhythm section with snare hit at the end of every turnaround.

Verse 1: The Lead vocal phrasing alternates with a strong bass-heavy riff and snare hit at the end of each vocal phrase. The pattern of Lead elements quickly becomes obvious: Lead vocal>riff and snare hit>Lead vocal>riff and snare hit.

Bridge 1: Lead vocal 'ooh-ooh's'.

Chorus: Lead vocal then at the end of the vocal phrase "...over you" there are four prominent kick drum hits.

Bridge: starting with the vocal phrase, "Yeah, I was dreamin' last night". The focus alternates between the Lead vocal, saxophone, bass with a picked electric guitar phrase and snare hits at the end of the section.
Note: Have a careful listen to this song and you'll hear the Lead continually change.

Sing – The Carpenters
A very well-crafted song with very strong vocal melody. At around 30 seconds in, note how the Lead vocal starts to alternate with short melodic instrumental phrases (Secondary Leads). These phrases provide momentum to the song by 'filling the holes' between each vocal phrase. The increase in melodic content seems to add 'pace' and interest to the song, and a contrast to the previous Verse.

Example of creating focus in a song

Song start: focus = Hook as guitar solo
Verse 1: focus = Lead vocal, then guitar riff Leading into Chorus 1
Chorus 1: focus = alternating main vocal and backing vocals, then horn section at end.
Verse 2: focus = Lead vocal, with guitar riffs between vocal lines, then drum fill at end.

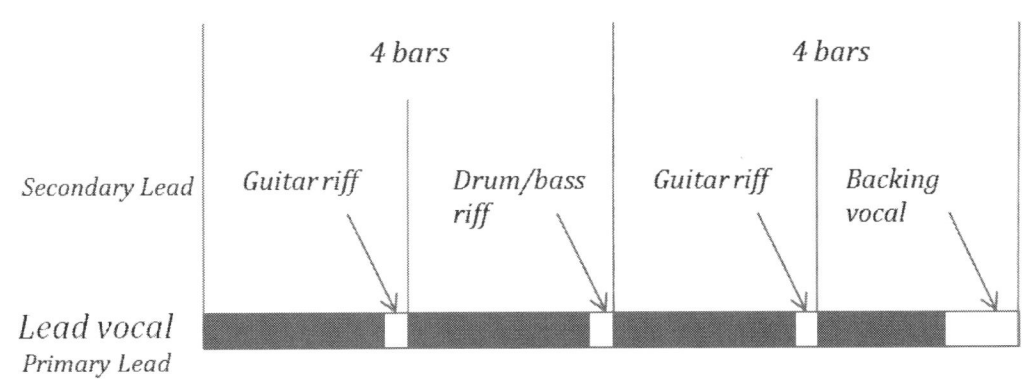

Chorus - 8 bar duration

Image G – Establishing the Lead in a Chorus
This image shows how a strong Lead can be created in a song by using a combination of Primary and Secondary Leads. The Lead vocal (Primary Lead) is supported by Secondary Leads that occur in the moments when the Lead vocal is not being sung.

The Primary Melody Rule

**A maximum of one Primary melody is
allowed at any one time in the song**

The Primary Melody Rule encapsulates the idea that there should only be one dominant melody playing at any one time. This doesn't stop us from creating interesting and colourful arrangements with multiple supporting melodies. It's a reminder to pick our 'main character' (Lead vocal, Lead instrument) and stick with it. The Rule doesn't prevent the introduction of a new Primary Melody, it just requires the song to only have one occurring at any given moment in the song. You can introduce a new main character (a guitar solo) later in the show if you like.

Competing melodies

The simultaneous occurrence of multiple strong melodies in a song can be confusing for listeners. Humans are sensitive to melodic information (particularly that which occurs in the most middle frequencies of the hearing range). If two or more melodies are delivered with similar timing and in the same frequency range the listener is faced with confusion. It's like having two people talk directly at you while you wonder who to listen to; one interrupts the other while the message of both is blurred.

During the arrangement process it's important to listen carefully for competing melodies. A common example is when a Lead vocal fights with a Lead guitar; when they're both playing together, with equal emphasis, it can be the equivalent of two instruments having an argument. The solution is much like a polite conversation; each one needs to let the other speak without interrupting.

Conversely, done well, multiple melodies can work in a song when one melodic element harmonically supports a primary melodic element. A very good example of this is in the Verses of Audioslave's 'Like A Stone'. A simple, repetitive Lead guitar melody harmonically supports the Lead vocal melody. The guitar's melody is simpler and its timing is slower than that of the vocal. In this example, the guitar line is purposely de-emphasised to allow the main melody to shine through.

To summarise, multiple melodies in a song can be engaging or problematic. Executed well, they can create colour and personality. Done poorly, they can render a song unlistenable.

Application

1. Find the 'holes' to establish the 'fills'
Finding the 'holes' is simple. First establish the Primary Lead then look for every gap in that Lead line. Often the Primary Lead is a Lead vocal, so the 'holes' are the gaps between each word or at the end of a phrase. Look for ways to tastefully 'fill' the 'holes' with Secondary Lead elements. The Rolling Stones' 'Emotional Rescue' is a great example of this.

2. Build energy
A great way to build energy is to introduce more Secondary Leads as the song progresses. It works to increase the number as the song progresses. Alternatively, create contrast by limiting the fills (Secondary Leads) in Verses and including lots in the Choruses.

3. Use frequency and transients
Select your fills based on their dominant frequency and transient information. Snare hits (heavily transient) and twangy guitar riffs (frequency prominent) are very obvious and 'ear-catching'. Bass riffs, softly played born lines and warm keyboard tones are less obvious. Select carefully for maximum effect.

4. Use the Primary Melody Rule to avoid competing melodies
A maximum of one primary melody is allowed at any one time.

5. Analyse popular songs
The song examples above provide good insight into the use of Primary and Secondary Lead combinations in a song. Consider how you might use the same principles to enhance your own arrangements.

13

Clarity and definition

Achieving clarity and definition of musical elements in the mix

Frequency masking caused by similar sounding musical elements can negatively impact mix clarity

The arrangement of musical elements in a song can have a big impact on the clarity of the final mix. When too many musical elements within a similar frequency range play simultaneously, masking occurs. Masking creates a lack of distinction between musical elements in the mix. The end result is that a Lead vocal may be difficult to hear because it's being masked by the electric guitars. The horn section may mask the warm Rhodes keyboard, and so on.

Masking naturally occurs when two elements with similar tonal qualities play simultaneously in a song. If only two elements are competing, this is fairly easy to address during mixing by applying EQ to alter the tonality of one element. If masking is excessive, the situation compounds, making it difficult to mix and negatively affecting the entire production.

The solution to this is twofold. Firstly, you need awareness of the issue. Secondly, you need the skills to select instrumentation that is tonally complementary. This doesn't mean changing the intentions of the songwriter, but rather, looking for tonal colour and variation in the intended instrumentation. This might be as simple as selecting a different guitar or changing pickups to achieve a guitar tone that supports the other guitars or reduces masking with the Lead vocal. When musical elements have distinctive tonality, the sonics of the finished song can have much more clarity.

Musical elements fall into the category of either 'transient' or 'tonal'

Transient element

These are musical elements with a naturally exaggerated initial transient spike. Some examples would be snare/kick/tom/tambourine/conga drum hits. Also single plucked electric guitars, sharply struck single piano notes, and vocal consonants, to name a few. Even though the sound has harmonic overtones from the construction and tuning of the drum, the dominant factor is its percussive nature.

Tonal element

These are musical elements identified by their sustained tonal character. Typical examples would be a flute, a keyboard pad, guitar strum, or sung vocal vowel.

It's quite common for elements to exhibit both transient and tonal qualities. One example is a single guitar note which is plucked hard with a hard pick; there is an initial transient then a sustained tone as the note rings out. Vocals also commonly exhibit similar transient/tonal qualities when words with hard consonants are sung with force. Words starting with K, T and P are obvious examples.

The arranger needs to be aware of the different types of elements and their transient and tonal qualities. This awareness allows a wider palate of choice when selecting and arranging musical elements in a song.

Balanced and engaging arrangements can be created when transient and tonal elements are placed evenly across the panoramic soundstage

There is real value in understanding how transient and tonal musical elements can help to create a balanced, vibrant and interesting song. Some genres are dominant in transient elements, such as heavily percussive Latin music. Hip-hop is a great example with its highly percussive rapping and dominant rhythms. In contrast, classical music is often less dominant in transients and more so in tonal sounds. Knowing how and where to use transient/tonal sounds can be a very powerful tool in affecting energy and excitement in a song.

Huge contrast can be created between sections in a song where Verses contain less transient and more tonal elements, transitioning into Choruses with a strong emphasis on both transient and tonal elements.

Imagine this pop song:

Verse:
Contains a softly played conga rhythm (low transient), accompanied by softly-played Rhodes keyboard (high tonal/low transient) and relaxed Lead vocalist (tonal and low transients from lightly pronounced consonants).

> *More transients equate to more intensity and energy*

Chorus:
Full drum kit (heavily transient), electric bass played with a pick (transient/tonal), electric rhythm guitar strummed with light-gauge pick (tonal), Rhodes played hard to accentuate the note attack (transient/tonal) and rapping vocalist (transient/tonal).

This example would present a low-energy and relaxed vibe in the Verse and a highly energetic Chorus. While the increase in volume of more instruments is partly the cause of the energy boost, an increase in intensity would be obvious due to the accentuation of transients in each of the musical elements.

Further enhancement can be achieved by panoramic position of the element relative to its dominant frequency range

The dominant frequency range of transient and tonal elements can be used as a guide for their panoramic positioning in the soundscape. The goal is to avoid having elements in similar frequency ranges competing in the same panoramic and frequency position in the final song. For example, locating an organ or electric guitar to the left or right to avoid masking the Lead vocal is important because these three elements can occupy the middle frequency range. Most care is required with the placement of mid-range frequency elements because there are often so many of these competing in a song's soundstage.

Example of song using transient and tonal elements across the frequency range

Let's consider the Chorus of a country rock song where the instruments are drums, electric bass, acoustic guitar, pedal guitar, violin and of course, Lead vocal. The diagram below shows these elements categorised into transient, tonal and frequency range.

Freq. Range	Transient	Tonal
Low	kick drum	bass
Low mid	Tom drums, xylophone	vocal
Mid	Snare drum, electric guitar (chick'n pick'n) xylophone, washboard	Vocal, acoustic guitar, pedal guitar, electric guitar (lead)
Mid high	tambourine	Vocal, violin (played in high register only)
High	Cymbals, triangle	Cymbals

Image H – Transient, Tonal and Frequency Characteristics of Song Elements

This analysis shows the relationship of transient, tonal and frequency characteristics of each element in the song. Doing such an analysis helps us to identify clashes (too many similar elements) and holes (missing elements) so that we can craft a song with a good distribution of transient and tonal elements across the full soundstage. It's immediately clear that there is a concentration of elements in the mid-range. This is often an area where the arranger needs to avoid excessive numbers of elements playing simultaneously due to the frequency masking issues that can result.

The reason this analysis was done for a Chorus rather than an entire song is that the makeup of musical elements can vary drastically in each song section. An analysis of a complete song would be limiting because it might show excessive mid-frequency elements (raising concerns about masking) that may actually be distributed quite evenly across the different song sections.

The clarity and definition of a song is affected by the tonal character of the musical elements within

Mix clarity can be improved when the number of competing elements is reduced

To enhance the clarity of an overall song and the definition of individual elements, we need to limit the number of elements playing at any one time. Imagine trying to hear one person talking in a large crowd. It's difficult or impossible due to the competing ambient noise in a similar frequency range caused by all the other people talking. Now imagine trying to hear that person if there are only three people – that single voice becomes more audible because there is less competition. Developing this idea further, we can achieve further clarity if only one person talks at a time. This same concept applies to the way musical elements compete within a mix; when similar sounding elements occur simultaneously they are more likely to lose distinction and clarity in the mix.

One of the simplest ways to add clarity to a song is to look for competing elements, prioritise the key ones and remove the rest. Sounds excessive? Of course it is. It can also result in beautifully clear, open mixes because there are less competing elements.

The important factor in the process of priority and removal is how we define 'competing element'. For example, do drums compete with vocals in terms of frequency range and transient/tonal characteristics? Not usually. Does a tambourine compete with a Rhodes organ using the same criteria? Unlikely! Does a Rhodes keyboard compete with the trombones in a horn section? Highly likely! Elements with similar frequency and transient/tonal characteristics only compete with each other when playing simultaneously.

A careful approach to arrangement would have:

1. Elements carefully selected and placed in the panoramic soundstage based on their frequency and transient/tonal characteristics.

2. No competing (frequency/transient/tonal) elements playing simultaneously in the song.

Digital multi-tracking encourages excessive track counts

Modern digital multi-tracking enables an almost limitless track-count during recording. There is a tendency to record more than is necessary because it gives more options later and allows a 'fix it in the mix' attitude.
While this approach has value when used sparingly (like recording clean versions of distorted guitars for later re-amping) it also creates a significant mixing job due to the shear multitude of tracks. Excessive tracks can also cause a 'muddy' or 'blurry' mix due to frequency masking and confusion for the audience due to the number of competing elements.

A thorough arrangement process would include careful planning to ensure that only the required musical elements are recorded.

The Element Placement Principle

A musical element's placement in the panoramic soundstage depends on its transient, tonal and frequency characteristics

The Element Placement Principle deals with the panoramic placement of elements in the soundstage based on their sound characteristics. Each element's sound characteristics dictate its placement. The goal of this principle is to reduce the occurrence of clashing elements and to create big, open and clear sounding song mixes. This principle is not limited to melodic elements, but covers all musical elements in a song's composition. Ideally, the principle would be applied to musical elements for each song section. This means you might use might create three; one for each of the Verses, Choruses and the Bridge in a song.

Looking more closely, the soundstage is divided into three <u>panoramic zones</u>: left, centre and right. Each panoramic zone is divided into three <u>frequency ranges:</u> low, mid and high. Within each frequency range, consideration is given to the transient or tonal characteristic of that element. This gives us nine possible <u>positions</u> to locate both transient and tonal elements in the song.

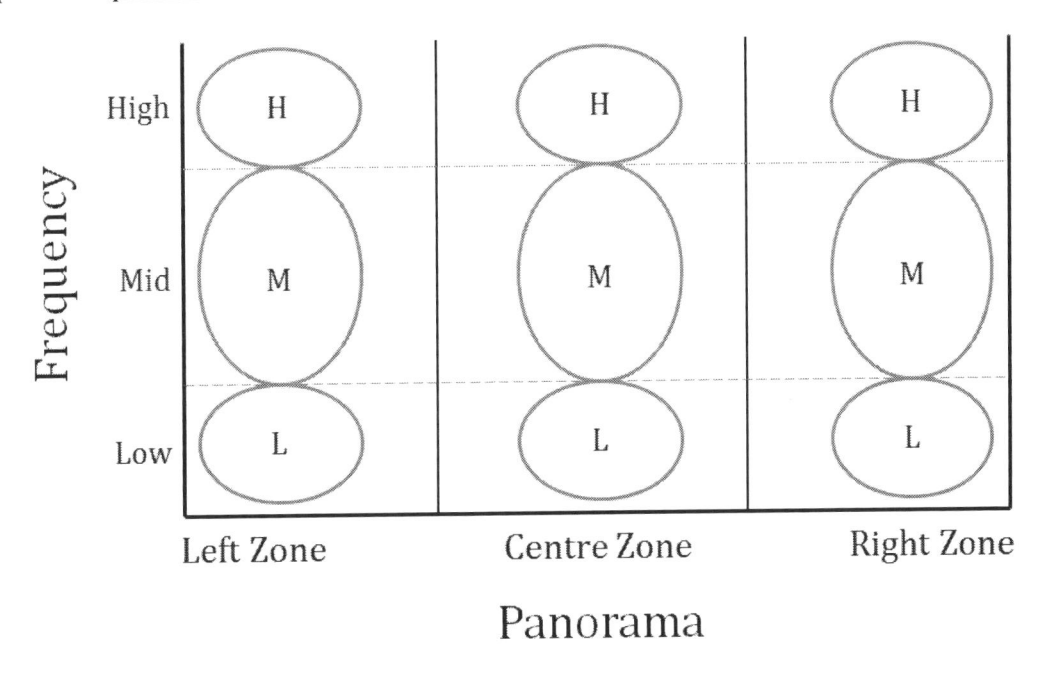

Image I – Zones and Frequency Ranges Within the Panoramic Soundstage

The goal during arrangement is to locate each musical element in the song, into one of the nine positions based on its transient or tonal characteristics. The panoramic zones are approximate; locating an element in the Left Zone doesn't mean a 'hard' pan left unless you want it that way. The frequency ranges are approximate too; a kick drum would normally live in the L position in the centre zone.

Each element is placed in the soundstage based on its sound characteristics:

1. Transient nature (e.g. drums, shakers, congas, hand-claps, vocal consonants etc.)

2. Tonal nature (e.g. guitars, pianos, strings, bass, keyboards, vocal vowels etc.)

3. Dominant frequency range (e.g. the occupying range of the element, for example, bass would be located in the L range)

Use an 'Element Placement Map' to locate the position of elements in terms of panorama and frequency

The primary goal of the Element Placement Map is to provide a visual reference for the Element Placement Principle. Using a visual guide makes it really easy to plan the arrangement and assist in avoiding clashes between musical elements with the same frequency range and transient/tonal characteristics. Ideally, one map would be created for each song section since the combinations of musical elements often change from section to section.

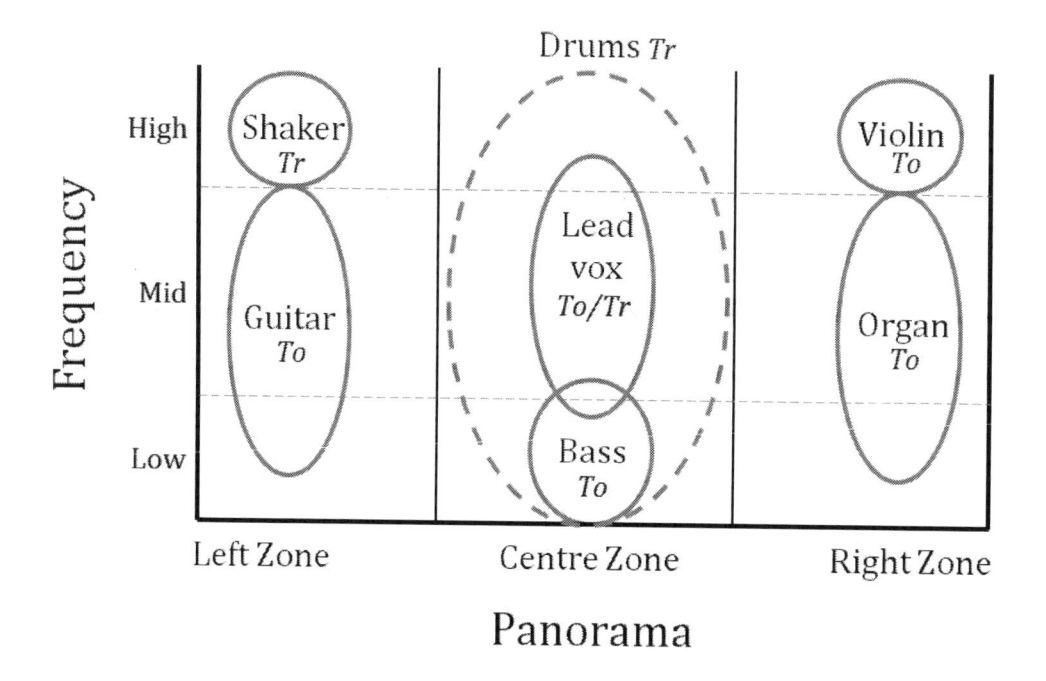

Image J – Element Placement Map for a Verse
This diagram shows the placement of elements based on their dominant frequency range and their tonal/transient characteristic. Elements with a 'To' mean the element is 'tonal', while elements with a 'Tr' mean 'transient'. The important part of this principle is to avoid positioning elements with the same sound characteristics in the same position. The drums show a dashed oval across all three frequencies to denote the kick, snare, toms and cymbals.
IMPORTANT: The Element Placement Map is only useful if it gets passed on to the mixing engineer so that element placement can be duplicated in the mix.

How to use The Element Placement Principle

1. Aim for a maximum of one <u>transient</u> element in any L, M or H positions.

2. Aim for a maximum of one <u>tonal</u> element in any L, M or H positions.

3. Put transient and tonal elements in the correct L, M or H positions relative to their dominant frequency.

4. A maximum of one transient and one tonal element can occupy any one position.

The goal of any principle or rule should be to understand it well enough to know when to successfully break it. As you work with the principle more, you will discover exceptions to the rule that are worth doing because they enhance the sound of the song.

Example of an acceptable combination:

The centre panoramic zone can have the drums (transient), bass (tonal, low frequency) and Lead vocal (tonal, mid frequency). In this example, there is only one transient component but two tonal elements. Two tonal components are not a problem because they occupy different frequency ranges.

Example of a problematic combination:

The left zone has an electric rhythm guitar (tonal, mid frequency) and an organ (tonal, mid frequency). There is a clash with two tonal, mid frequency elements occupying the same zone.

Panoramic placement can be fine-tuned by considering the depth position of elements

In the same way that panoramic placement can be roughly divided up into left, centre and right, the depth position can be considered in a similar way, being front, middle and rear. Considering depth in such simple terms makes it easy to decide on a depth position because there are only three to choose from.

Limiting ourselves to three also means that the delay-based effects used to achieve these positions can be much more obvious to the listener. Finally, it allows the arranger to easily consider the three-dimensional soundstage of the song. This can lead to questions like, where is the Lead vocalist relative to the drum kit? Does the string ensemble sit at the rear? In which of the three depth positions does each of the song elements live?

The amount of delay-based effect (like reverb and delays) applied defines the depth of the element. A front depth position would have a very dry/minimal effect. A middle depth position would have a moderate effect, with rear position incurring a strong reverb.

The value of a simple method to design depth placement is that if you combine it with the Element Placement Principle, a rich range of opportunities are possible in terms of both width and depth placement of elements in a mix. For the arithmetically-minded among us, that's 9 x 3 = 27 potential positions for musical elements in the song soundstage.

Altering the tonality of an instrument is an effective way to create definition between competing instruments

This is best done at the time of recording because the tonal variations achievable can be vast compared to trying to alter during the mixing process. Comparing instrument tonality during recording allows us to capture varying tones that will enhance the final mix. This is useful when recording multiple versions of any musical element and particularly with mid-range elements like vocals, guitars, keyboards and horns.

If we are recording two similar guitar tracks, big variations in tonality can be achieved by different effects pedals, changing amps, mic placement and even simply changing the pickup selection (my favourite). Similarly, a change in microphone, preamp or mic position can provide a variation in tonal quality that can comfortably separate a Lead vocal from a backing vocal in the song recording.

When similar sounding elements occur simultaneously they are more likely to lose distinction and clarity in the mix

When our goal is to create definition for the elements in the mix, we can start asking ourselves questions like:

1. What's the key musical phrase that should be emphasised in this part of the song?

2. How can I get this phrase to achieve dominance and clarity in the mix?

3. Is this key phrase being supported or hindered by the other musical elements?

4. How does each musical phrase playing right now, support the song?

5. All of these musical elements playing simultaneously: are they all necessary?

The Polaroid Principle

Each element should have its own state of focus to enable depth and balance in the overall song soundscape

The Polaroid Principle enables the creation of depth, focus and balance in a song recording. The Principle allows you to conceptualise a song's soundscape much like you might see a range of physical elements in a photograph.

A sensitive photographer can focus sharply on a key element in the scene while blurring the less important elements using 'depth of field' in the camera lens. The ability to capture an entire scene and focus on a key element enables the photographer to create a stage where the surrounding out-of-focus elements add context and balance to the main element.

In comparison, modern, cheap, digital cameras can place everything in focus and in doing so, leave the key element up to the viewer. The comparison with music is that an 'all-elements-in-focus' approach doesn't guide the listener's ear in the same way that 'depth of field' guides a viewer's eye.

The Polaroid Principle can be immensely helpful during arrangement because it enables you to conceptualise a soundstage where there is distinction between the elements in focus and those that are blurred.

How do we create focus or blurring of elements in the song production?

Problem: modern high quality digital recording technology coupled with an appropriate recording chain enables the capture of pristine audio quality. The result is that all recorded elements can be 'highly focused'. When the elements are assembled into a song the mixing engineer can use simple processing to reduce focus, like reducing high frequency content or applying reverb to create depth. Alternatively the elements can be recorded with a 'reduced focus' tonal quality in mind by recording 'warmer', less strident tones. Whatever process is used, it's important to have a clear intention about the tonal quality of all elements and how this contributes to the amount of focus in the final soundscape.

Simple techniques to reduce the focus (blur) of a musical element

1. Apply a low pass filter
It's natural for high frequencies to reduce as the listener moves further from the source. Applying a LPF (low pass filter) removes high frequencies and simulates distance. This is a very effective treatment for blurring vocals, as much of the clarity from consonants (B, P, K, T), fricatives and esses is in the higher frequencies.

2. Apply EQ to remove frequencies in the sensitive hearing range
Fletcher Munson's Equal Loudness Contour Curve shows frequency ranges where our ears are naturally very sensitive. For example, our ears are sensitive to frequencies in the 2 kHz to 5 kHz range and applying EQ reduction in this range can reduce the clarity of any element. (Any quick internet search will bring up an image of the Fletcher Munson Equal Loudness Contour Curve).

3. Apply reverb
Applying reverb has the effect of placing an element further from the listener or in other words, deeper into the mix. This effect can be accentuated if a LPF is also applied.

4. Lower the volume
This is the simplest of all techniques. When an element is lower in volume than its competing elements, it loses clarity.

5. Reduce transients
Elements that are rich in transients are more exciting to the ear and generally call attention to themselves. Transient reduction can be done by applying fast compression to reduce the initial transients. Also, selecting 'soft' sounding elements like a keyboard pad, a gently strummed guitar or backing vocals with limited consonants (like 'oohs' and 'aahs') works because they have less exaggerated initial transients. Playing any stringed instrument softly is very effective, such as playing a bass line with fingers instead of a pick.

Simple techniques to increase the focus of a musical element

1. Raise the volume
The simplest method to add focus is to turn it up! Obviously it's only effective if the volume increase puts the element louder than competing elements. However, frequency masking and varying levels reduce the effectiveness of this simple technique.

2. Apply compression
Applying compression results in raising the average volume of the musical element. This means that more quietly played parts of a musical phrase are now louder, resulting in more prominence.

3. Apply EQ
It's reasonably well known that a reduction or increase in the right frequency ranges will help to make an element more distinct. The key is to know first what you are trying to achieve before twiddling the knobs. For example, improving a Lead vocal's intelligibility can often be improved by a gentle EQ lift in the 5 kHz to 10 kHz range.

4. Remove or reduce the volume of competing elements
Clarity is very much a relative issue. In other words, raising the volume of a vocal in a song recording has the same effect as lowering the volume of competing elements. Either method achieves the same goal but affects the overall balance of the song soundscape. The simplest approach is simply to mute competing elements so that the most important element can be heard clearly. Alternatively, volume automation allows much finer control when balancing a range of elements simultaneously.

Application

1. Use the 'Element Placement Principle' to avoid clashing and create clarity
Locate musical elements in a song's panoramic soundstage based on their sound characteristics: transient, tonal and dominant frequency.

2. Create an 'Element Placement Map' to visualise the placement of elements
The Element Placement Map allows you to visualise decisions made using the Element Placement Principle. It's best to create one map for each song section as the arrangement of elements can change from Verse to Chorus. Providing the Element Placement Map to the mixing engineer ensures that the placement decisions are kept intact and end up in the final mix.

3. Create depth in the soundscape using delay-based effects
Use delay-based effects to help you locate the depth position of elements: front, middle, or rear. Depth placement decisions are only useful if passed on to the mixing engineer.

4. Use the 'Polaroid' Principle
This principle helps you visualise a soundscape of musical elements much like a photographer sees a range of physical objects in a scene; some are sharply in focus while others are blurred. Thinking about what musical elements are blurred or in focus at any one time enables us to apply treatment accordingly.

5. Analyse popular songs
Listen to popular songs and analyse the way musical elements are located in the song's soundscape, such as:
a) the number of musical elements playing at any one time (consider the drums as one element).
b) the location of elements in the panoramic soundstage.
c) how much clarity and definition is in the mix based on the selection of elements playing at any one time.
d) which elements are 'out of focus' and which are 'in focus'.

14

Symmetry and repetition

How patterns, repetition and variation affect the song arrangement

Controlled pattern symmetry helps create a solid arrangement

When a musical phrase is repeated consistently without variation, we experience 'symmetry' in the performance. In the case of a one-bar rhythm pattern, symmetry might be achieved by all the drum elements or just the kick drum. With tonal elements, like a bass guitar groove, symmetry could be created by consistent timing even though the melodic phrasing changes. To take this idea further, a typical song would likely have varying symmetry in each section. In the example of our kick drum, a simple pattern might be done in the Verses and a more complex pattern in the Choruses. In short, symmetry can be achieved by a consistently repeated phrasing (timing) or melody.

The big question, of course, is how does this contribute to a good arrangement? While symmetry is useful when it's consistent, it also gets rather boring if it never varies in a song. That might suit some songs like Hip-hop, where a repeating rhythm is a signature sound of that genre. However, controlled variation of symmetry in a song helps build a professional sound to the song. For example, if all Verses have a consistent symmetry to the drum and bass performance, our audience can get a cue that they're now in the Verse, before the vocal even starts. Consistency builds familiarity and we want our listeners to feel our songs are familiar.

During the arrangement process, it's important to be aware of performance consistency and how pattern variations contribute to the quality of the song. It may be that a lack of consistency in a song's sections is the goal. However, the goal is to be aware of symmetry and repetition in the performance of musical parts. When you're aware, you can take control and make decisions about the performance.

Performance Repetition: macro and micro

At a macro or big-picture level, performance repetition refers to how and when sections are repeated throughout a song. At a micro level it is about the repetition of musical phrases in a sequence.

Repetition at the Macro level

A song can quickly become boring and predictable for a listener when the same sounding sections are repeated too often in sequence; too little and the song might fail to develop continuity and familiarity for the listener. The goal for the arranger is to achieve a balance between too much and too little.

The big question is how to strike the optimum balance of section repetition in a song. The popular song format of AABAABCBB shows this (A is a Verse, B is a Chorus, C is a Bridge), where no section is repeated more than twice in sequence before it changes.

When we get the balance right, our listeners quickly gain familiarity with the song due to the repeating sections, but they don't get bored with the song from over-repetition. Ideally, at the end of the song, we want the listeners to feel familiar with the song and remember the Hook.

Repetition at the Micro Level

Repetition at the micro level is about the patterns of rhythm, melody, harmony, and phrasing within song sections. It's a consideration of how these elements repeat both individually and in combination, and how they interact. In its simplest form it means getting the right balance of repetition for a single element, like a drum pattern in a Verse. Getting the right balance means using enough repetition to anchor the performance, but not so much that it becomes rigid and boring. In its more complex form, Repetition involves the manipulation and interaction of many patterns and musical elements in a song.

An example of complex form might have an 8-bar Verse with a combination of a Lead vocal, a bass, guitar, and drums. Even though each element has its own unique pattern of repetition, it combines with the others to form a cohesive whole. In other words, lots of smaller patterns combine to create larger, more complex patterns. While this might sound complex, it's something many songs exhibit quite naturally. However, the big question is whether pattern combinations are done well and how they contribute to making a better song. As arrangers, we need to be aware of what it is we're doing, and why we're doing it, versus doing stuff in autopilot mode without a reason.

Consider a 1-bar drum pattern that's repeated eight times to form an 8-bar Verse. The drummer plays a 'straight' kick/snare pattern with 8th note timing on the hi-hats. If the drummer plays precisely the same pattern every time it quickly gets boring due to the lack of variation. However, in this example our drummer introduces a variation by opening the hi-hat at the end of the second turnaround. The drummer returns to the original pattern for the third turnaround. At the end of the fourth turnaround, the drummer adds an extra kick and a light flam on the snare.

These small variations in the repeating pattern are adding interest for the listener without massively altering the fundamental beat – potentially a good thing. This pattern looks like this: ABAC. What this pattern achieves is consistency *and* variety; a good thing. Achieving a happy balance between consistency and variety is important in achieving success with pattern manipulation.

Achieving a happy balance between consistency and variety is key to the success of pattern manipulation

The Rule of Two

An identical musical section or phrase is not repeated more than twice in a sequence without a variation or change on the third time

There is a common trait in many popular songs that I term, The Rule of Two. While The Rule of Two is not a hard-and-fast rule to be found in every song, its occurrence in radio hits is so common and its application so useful, that it warrants a simple way to remember it. Using The Rule of Two will help you avoid excessive repetition in every aspect of the song; from melodic Hooks to the arrangement of sections. It will help ensure there is enough repetition to build familiarity for listeners while keeping the song fresh and never boring. This is a very effective rule which, consistently applied, can improve the results in every aspect of your arrangements.

The Rule of Two can be applied to every part of a song; from the macro to the micro; for sections and elements. The Rule is often effective with a Lead vocal because the variation reduces 'listener saturation' that occurs when highly melodic content is repeated too often.

The most important aspect of The Rule of Two is about knowing when to break it. In other words, apply it rigorously and critically while looking for times when it does not produce the desired results. This often means relaxing the Rule for the vocal phrasing and melody during a Chorus; allowing four repetitions of the vocal Hook. This works because more repetition is often one of the requirements of a Hook.

The following diagrams show The Rule of Two being applied at both a macro (song) and micro (element) level. For maximum value, focus on how small patterns combine into larger, more complex patterns. Also, pay attention to how pattern sequence affects consistency and variation.

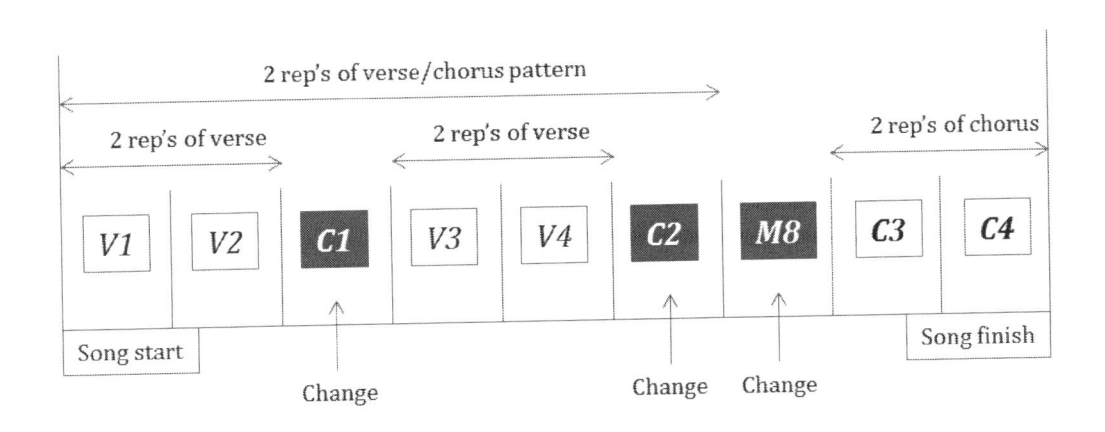

Image K – The Rule of Two Applied to a Song Format
This image shows a pattern of repetition within a song's timeline where no section or combination of sections is repeated more than twice. Note the 'change' section (Chorus) occurring at the end of each two Verse repetitions. Most importantly, notice the patterns within patterns that are created by the VVC combination being broken by the Middle-8.

```
| V1 | 8 bars    | V2 | 8 bars    | B1 | 8 bars                    C1
```

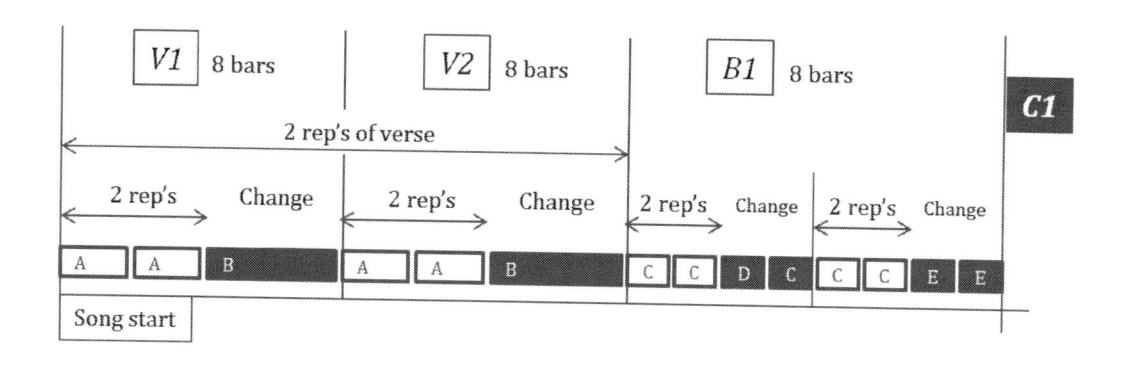

Image L – The Rule of Two Applied to a Vocal Delivery
This image shows the pattern of vocal repetitions across the first two Verses and Bridge in a song's timeline. Each block indicates one complete turnaround of a melodic phrase with each one shown by a box with a letter inside; a different letter denotes a different phrase. The phrases differ in length between the Verse and the Bridge. The key point is that change occurs after two repetitions of a phrase.

More examples of The Rule of Two

1. A Verse/Chorus cycle is repeated only twice before moving to a different section, such as a Bridge. This is shown in the common song format of ABABCBB where A is a Verse, B is a Chorus and C is the Bridge. Variation occurs in the third iteration.

2. A drummer plays a hi-hat lift at the end of the second turnaround and a variation on the kick and snare at the end of the fourth.

3. In a Verse, a Lead vocalist sings two repetitions of a melodic phrase with a variation or change on the third.

Examples of The Rule of Two in famous radio hits

<u>Don't Stop Till You Get Enough – Michael Jackson</u>
The first two Lead vocal lines repeat with the same melody and phrasing. The third repetition starting with "Power" includes a variation from the added lyrics "Ah the power". The vocals then continue with a very similar melody, but with a variation on the third occurrence before moving to the Chorus. The Chorus vocals depart from The Rule of Two with a 4 x repetition of the Chorus vocal Hook.

You Belong With Me – Taylor Swift
The melody of the first two vocal lines repeats twice, then changes on the third starting with "she doesn't get your humour like I do". This AAB vocal pattern repeats and then moves to a Bridge section. The Bridge section has an AABC + DDEE format for vocal phrasing. The song then moves to the Chorus section. The format of the vocal phrasing within the sections looks like this (note that the bar length for each phrase varies):
Verse 1 – AAB, Verse 2 – AAB, Bridge – AABC, DDEE, Chorus - AABB

This Is How We Roll – Florida Georgia Line
The melody of the first two vocal lines repeats twice, then changes on the third repetition starting with "Truck's jacked up...", before progressing to the Chorus.

Alive – Pearl Jam
Again, the vocal melody repeats twice, with a change on the third starting with, "sorry you didn't see him...". The vocal Hook in the Chorus occurs three times before a variation. It is reasonably common to break the 'Rule of Two' pattern to emphasize the Chorus Hook. The format for the vocal melody looks like this:
Verse – AAB AAB, Bridge – AA, Chorus – AAAB

Application

1. Apply The Rule of Two to keep a song fresh and interesting
Apply The Rule of Two to the repetition of song sections and song elements. Keep the arrangement fresh and alleviate the potential boredom of repetition and predictability. Most importantly, know when to break the rule.

2. Focus on patterns
Arrangement is the process of creating and organising interesting and engaging pattern combinations for your listeners. Your goal is to manage the repetition of song sections, melody and phrasing.

3. Pay attention to Symmetry
Consider the Symmetry created by the phrasing of song elements: drum beats, bass lines, rhythm instruments and Lead elements. Good Symmetry = controlled consistency. Try and achieve a fine balance between Symmetry and Variation.

4. Analyse popular songs
Look out for the Symmetry and Repetition used in popular songs. There are fascinating and common patterns that emerge; The Rule of Two is one of those common patterns.

Here are some questions you can ask yourself when analysing popular songs:
a) How often does each section repeat before it changes to a new section?
b) How many times does the Lead vocal melody and/or phrasing repeat before it changes?
c) How many times do other elements (drums/bass/guitar etc.) repeat before changing?
d) What kind of phrasing patterns form inside the sections, like the example shown in Image L above?

15

Comparison and analysis

Analyse and compare your arrangements with popular songs in the same genre

Analysis is HUGELY powerful in developing your arrangement skills

Analysing popular songs can provide huge insight into the techniques used by the pros. Once you understand these techniques you can implement them into your own songs. As you start analysing, you'll start to see techniques that are regularly used. For example, pop and rock songs often follow similar formats like ABABCBB. The TTC (Time-To-Chorus) is often around 30 – 45 seconds and a song's duration is around 3.30. The Rule of Two is often applied and then broken at Choruses, where repetition of the Hook becomes important. These are just a few common ones. As you start scrutinising, patterns will emerge, common techniques will become obvious, and certain techniques will resonate with you. The best advice to make this process worthwhile, is to record your findings. Write them down in an 'arrangement journal' and refer to them often as you develop your skills.

Comparing your songs to professional songs can improve your arrangements

Any song that has made its way onto a billboard is evidence of massive popularity.

Two worthwhile questions to ask are:

1. What is it about the song that has universal appeal?

2. How can I use these techniques to improve my own songs?

To properly analyse a popular song requires a list of criteria to measure against. This is useful on a number of levels. Firstly, it provides a solid basis of direct questions. Secondly, using the same criteria for analysing lots of songs allows comparison of the results. The goal of comparing the results is to look for common patterns which you can use in your own arrangements. For instance, if most radio hits reach the Chorus within 45 seconds, with a total duration of 3.30, then you could emulate these features in your own songs, assuming that your own songs are destined for radio.

Let's start analysing and comparing

You could get started immediately by doing a general analysis of popular songs in a specific genre and covering a certain period. For example, a study of number one radio hits in the genre of rock, for the period of the 1980s. You could analyse 30 songs; that's three number one hits per year. Remember that the goal of this exercise is to reveal common patterns that can be used as a rule-book for your own arrangements.

Another method is to compare a current song of your own with a popular song in the same genre. In this case the goal is to compare the differences between the two songs and look for ways to alter your song to reflect the features that you like from the popular song.

Whichever method you use, you will find that enough time spent doing analysis and comparison will improve your knowledge and understanding of professional arrangements. You will likely discover other areas of interest, such as the stylistic differences in arrangements between artists, genres and the arrangers/producers involved.

An arrangement editing exercise

The aim of this exercise is to create different arrangements from an existing song, with the goal of finding the most appealing arrangement. You can use an existing popular song recording or one of your own.

Steps:

1. Open a DAW session and import one song file.

2. Separate the song into its individual sections and output/render a separate audio file of each section. Save these into a new folder and name it 'song sections'. Name the files for each section e.g. Intro, Verse 1, Verse 2, Chorus 1, Chorus 2, Bridge, Outro etc.

3. Now the fun starts. The goal is to create different versions of the original arrangement. Doing this in a new DAW session prevents you from cheating by referring to the original.

Import the section files you saved earlier and re-arrange them to create at least three different arrangements. Your aim is to create what you believe is the best structure for the song. After you're done, render each new arrangement and burn them to a CD or create MP3 files. Listen to them on your mobile device, in the car or send them to your peers for discussion.

This method becomes more difficult if you use a song you're not familiar with AND you do the re-arrangement some weeks later; by that time you will likely have forgotten the original arrangement.

The best approach to honing your arranging skills is the 'learning-by-doing' method

There's no disputing that enough focused time spent honing your skills will get you closer to being an expert. However, many small studios either don't have the quantity of projects coming through, or the clients with sufficient budget for arrangement services. One solution to getting lots of projects is to join online mixing forums like www.mixoff.org and www.indaba.com. While you might be working for free, you can experience significant improvements in a very short time. For example, you could commit to the re-arrangement and remix of two songs per week. If that doesn't sound like much, try sticking with this for one year. You will experience gains like never before and you'll have chalked up over 100 projects, or 10 albums. That's a big deal for a small studio.

Analysing a song's arrangement

Research is far more powerful when you keep a record of the things you discover then do something useful with the findings. Use a method that's easy and convenient to record your findings, like a small paper journal or mobile device. If you reflect regularly on your findings, you might start to form your own opinions, rules and guidelines that you can use for your own arrangements.

10 questions for analysing an arrangement

1. What is the total song duration in minutes and seconds?

2. What is the song tempo in BPM (beats per minute)?

3. What is the TTC (time from start to first Chorus)?

4. At what time (in seconds) is the Hook first introduced and then re-introduced?

5. What is the song's structure or format? (AABA).

6. How does song energy relate to each section? Create a Dynamics Map.

7. What is the Key of the song?

8. How many times does a song section repeat before changing? Is The Rule of Two used?

9. What are the Lead elements in each section and when do they occur?

10. What does online research tell you about why the song is so popular?

10 questions for analysing popular songs

1. What are the number-one pop hits for each year for the last five years?

2. What are the number-one billboard hits in other genres such as classical, alternative, indie, country, jazz for example? Are there characteristics that are common across all of these genres?

3. What are the most famous hits from prominent older artists (The Beatles, Pink Floyd, Elvis etc.) and what are the similar characteristics of these songs that gives them appeal.

4. What are your own personal all-time favourite songs? Are there common characteristics that appeal to you?

5. Is there a similarity between the order of sections for hit songs?

6. What are reoccurring features between the radio hits across the years?

7. How does the arrangement differ for different genres?

8. Do complex arrangements make a song more or less *accessible*?

9. Sketch a Dynamics Map of popular songs and compare.

10. Analyse how Builds are incorporated into Verses and Choruses of popular songs.

16 Checklist

Song Arrangement Checklist

Date: ....

Song Name: ....

Artist: ....

Genre: ....

Audience/Destination: ....

Duration: ....

TTC (Time-To-Chorus): ....

Rules and Principles

The Rule of Two

An identical musical section or phrase is not repeated more than twice in a sequence without a variation or change on the third time

The Primary Melody Rule

A maximum of one Primary melody is allowed at any one time in the song

The Element Placement Principle

A musical element's placement in the panoramic soundstage depends on its transient, tonal and frequency characteristics

The Polaroid Principle

Each element should have its own state of focus to enable depth and balance in the overall song soundscape

Song Arrangement for the Small Recording Studio

Dynamics Map (show location of Hooks, builds, and Transitions):

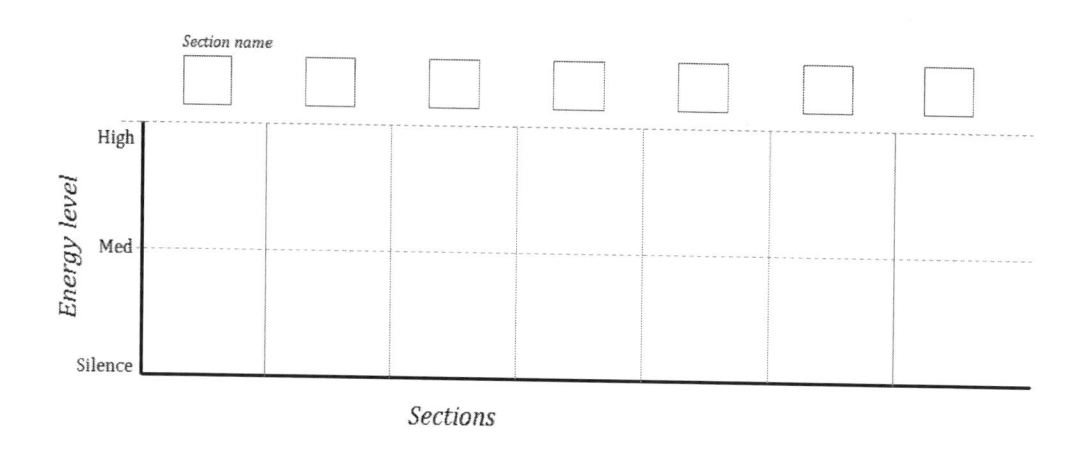

Section name

Energy level: High, Med, Silence

Sections

Element Placement Map
Show the placement of musical based on their frequency range and transient/tonal characteristics. Ideally, one map would be created for each song section.

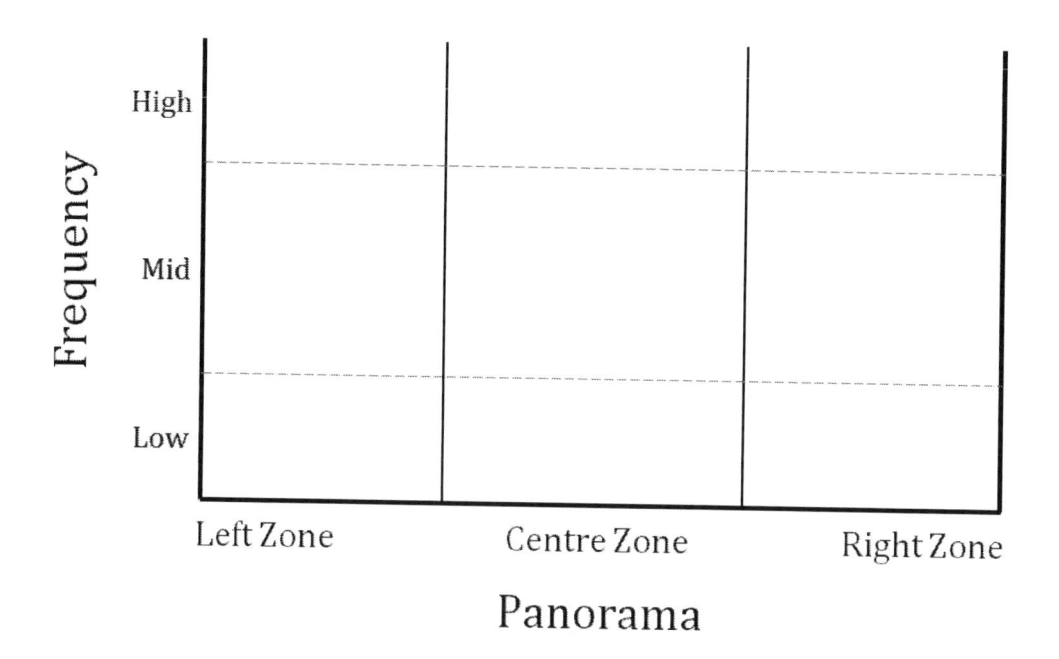

Frequency: High, Mid, Low

Panorama: Left Zone, Centre Zone, Right Zone

17 Glossary

Bridge
The term Bridge can be confusing as it can refer to two quite different types of musical sections. The traditional idea of a Bridge is a short musical section to connect two longer musical sections, such as a short transitionary section between a Verse and Chorus. A more modern reference to a Bridge makes it synonymous with a Middle-8, which is a musical section used later in a song to add contrast and break up the repetitive pattern of the song.

Build
The addition and/or variation of musical elements to add interest and a change in energy to repeating song sections.

DAW
Digital Audio Workstation. This is the recording and mixing software on your computer.

Dynamics Map
A visual representation of the dynamic energy flow across all sections in a song. The X axis shows all sections in the song in the correct order. The Y axis measures the subjective or perceived level of song energy, where zero = no musical elements and no volume, low = low energy, medium = medium energy, high = high energy.

Element (musical)
A musical part or phrase created by an individual instrument or vocal.

Interlude
A short musical piece between sections in a musical arrangement.

Lead element
The Lead element is a single musical element or group of elements that holds the main focus for the listener at any one time. They are divided into Primary Leads and Secondary Leads. Primary Lead is a prominent Lead element, such as a Lead vocal or a Lead solo. Secondary Leads are usually short musical phrases that occur in the gaps of a Lead phrase. They can also occur simultaneously with the Lead melody but be sufficiently de-emphasised to provide a supporting role to the Lead (such as the Verse guitar melody in Audioslave's 'Like A Stone').

Middle-8
A section of a musical arrangement that occurs later in the song and is usually around eight bars in duration. It often consists of a different melody, chord sequence, rhythm or a combination of these. Its function is to add contrast to the song by breaking up the repetitive pattern of a typical song structure. It is also referred to as a Bridge.

Phrase
A short piece of a musical performance by an individual instrument or vocal.

Pre-Chorus
A short piece of music, commonly 2 – 4 bars in duration, used to join a Verse and a Chorus section. Sometimes referred to as a Bridge.

Section – *musical section*
This book refers to sections as major parts in a musical arrangement. They include the Intro, Verse, Pre-Chorus, Chorus, Bridge, Middle-8 and Outro.

Tonal Element
Tonal elements are characterised by their sustained or slowly decaying sound, such as a held organ chord, a strummed guitar chord, or held note on a flute. Although the musical element must be capable of creating the sustained sound, whether the final recorded sound is Tonal or Transient, is much to do with how it is played. For example, while an organ can play a sustained chord (Tonal), it can also be played in a very percussive style, making the end product more Transient in nature. Examples of tonal elements include strings, a sung vocal note, a sustained note or chord from a guitar, a held organ, and horns.

Transient Element
A Transient element is a sound with a strong percussive attack as its main sound characteristic. Viewing a Transient sound in an audio editor will show a strong peak at the front of its waveform. In this book it is often used in direct comparison to a Tonal element (refer to Tonal Element in this glossary). Some examples of Transient elements are drum hits, strong consonants or 'plosives' in a vocal, percussion, hand-claps, plucked and muted guitar notes.

Transition
The purpose of a Transition is to signal to the listening audience, the progression from one song section to the next. It comprises a variation to existing, or introduction of new, musical elements and is usually included within the musical section, rather than as a new section. For example, a Transition might occur in the last bar or two of a Verse leading into a Chorus.

TTC (Time-To-Chorus)
This is a measurement of the time in seconds from the very start of the song to the start of the first Chorus.

Thanks

Well, you got this far – well done!

I want to offer you a very big thanks for reading this book. I sincerely hope you found value in it. This book can serve as a useful reference as you try the different techniques and ideas and further develop your own song arrangement skills and techniques.

I would really appreciate it if you could leave me a positive review on Amazon with your honest comments and feedback. I read all the feedback and use your comments with future revisions and other books.

Sincerely
Amos Clarke

Other books by the author

The books are available on Amazon.com in both Kindle and paperback format.

Macro-Mixing for the Small Recording Studio
Produce better mixes, faster than ever using simple techniques that actually work

Macro-Mixing For The Small Recording Studio is intended for beginner and intermediate mixing engineers who want to find new ways to massively improve their workflow and the quality of their studio mixes. The book is packed with techniques, examples, guides, and tips to help you create a 'breakthrough' with your mixing. The author includes anecdotes from his own experience working with bands and working on mixing projects.

56 Mix Tips for the Small Recording Studio
Practical techniques to take your mixes to the next level

Create magic in your mixes. Flip to any page, read the technique, and apply it. It's really that simple. This is not a book that trawls relentlessly through the world history of mixing before providing any useful advice. It simply gets straight into the business of giving you real tried and proven mixing tips that actually work. And there's plenty to keep you busy. The book covers processing such as compression, equalization, panning, parallel compression, transient manipulation, harmonic distortion, delay based effects and much more.

Made in the USA
Middletown, DE
16 May 2017